AWAKENING:
our soul journeys

The Aquarian Team

BALBOA.
PRESS

A DIVISION OF HAY HOUSE

Balboa Press books may be ordered through booksellers or by contacting:

Balboa Press
A Division of Hay House
1663 Liberty Drive
Bloomington, IN 47403
www.balboapress.com
1 (877) 407-4847

Because of the dynamic nature of the Internet, any web addresses or
links contained in this book may have changed since publication and
may no longer be valid. The views expressed in this work are solely those
of the author and do not necessarily reflect the views of the publisher,
and the publisher hereby disclaims any responsibility for them.

The author of this book does not dispense medical advice or prescribe
the use of any technique as a form of treatment for physical, emotional,
or medical problems without the advice of a physician, either directly
or indirectly. The intent of the author is only to offer information
of a general nature to help you in your quest for emotional and
spiritual well-being. In the event you use any of the information in
this book for yourself, which is your constitutional right, the author
and the publisher assume no responsibility for your actions.

Any people depicted in stock imagery provided by Thinkstock are
models, and such images are being used for illustrative purposes only.
Certain stock imagery © Thinkstock.

Print information available on the last page.

ISBN: 978-1-5043-6603-8 (sc)
ISBN: 978-1-5043-6602-1 (e)

Balboa Press rev. date: 12/02/2016

CONTENTS

FOREWORD

What direction is my life taking? What lasting effects will my choices and actions have on this world? Questions such as these become important in almost everyone's life at some point or other.

The testimonies in this book show that human beings who go through an awakening of consciousness are capable of transforming themselves, of becoming happier, more dynamic, more complete and even more beautiful—because an interior transformation inevitably manifests itself on one's face. The authors of these stories tell us how they have experienced a powerful awakening after discovering the Teaching of a spiritual Master. The birth of that new consciousness, sometimes like a bolt of lightning, sometimes in a slow succession of waves, has led each of them to a profound transformation in their philosophy of life, in their conduct.

What is this Teaching, and who is this spiritual Master, Omraam Mikhaël Aïvanhov?

One could answer both questions in the same breath. This Master, who spent his entire life enlightening and helping his fellow men and women, is really *one* with the Teaching he transmitted. On the one hand he presents, with a new vision, the most elevated ideas that are part of humanity's spiritual heritage. On the other hand, being an exceptional philosopher, he sheds a new and invigorating light on the simplest aspects of our lives. Finally, he offers easy and efficient methods which can help us as we address our daily problems, and these methods are perfectly adapted to our times.

Personally, I discovered his philosophy of life about forty years ago, and the new concepts I became familiar with gave me such powerful spiritual energies that my whole life changed color and texture. I read all his books one after the other, like a person dying of thirst after spending years in the desert.

A year later, when I had the privilege of meeting him at his spiritual school, *Le Bonfin*, I knew in my happiness that from then on my whole life would be inspired by his Teaching. I was captivated by the methods and suggestions he gave us in order that we might nourish ourselves with light, feed our physical and subtle bodies and find in Nature all the elements for our physical and spiritual survival and wellbeing.

"Learn to find nourishment in light," he used to say, "for in doing so you will find the greatest possible blessings; you will feel so rich that you will begin to love every creature."[1] When he explained that love is *a state of consciousness*, it was finally clear for me that love should impregnate all the events of my life, even the humblest ones. "When it becomes more intense," he said, "love is compelled to manifest as light."[2] The only thing I wanted was to walk on this path of light, which is the path of unconditional love.

Much later, when he had already left this world, some extraordinary circumstances led me to begin a long period of research in order to write his biography. I wasn't even a writer by then, but a painter and an art teacher. Throughout the seven years it took me to do this exacting, difficult but wondrous work, I could appreciate how fully Omraam Mikhaël Aïvanhov lived what he taught. This became obvious as I studied his life, reading over 2,500 of his lectures, interviewing some hundred witnesses and gathering information in Bulgaria, his country of birth.

"He was my best friend and my spiritual Master." These words, addressed to me by an elderly man I interviewed in Bulgaria, express perfectly what a good number of Mikhaël's acquaintances had felt about him in his youth. Between the

---

[1]   Omraam Mikhaël Aïvanhov, *Light is a Living Spirit*, Prosveta.

[2]   Omraam Mikhaël Aïvanhov, *The Living Book of Nature*, Prosveta.

age of seventeen and thirty-seven, he lived at the heart of the brotherhood created by the spiritual Master Peter Deunov. During that time, Mikhaël tried to remain in the background, but people sought his company, wanting to take part in his spiritual experiences and to seek his advice.

After his arrival in France, where he went at Peter Deunov's request to establish a branch of the Bulgarian Brotherhood, he was a living example of the teaching he was transmitting and which he would develop over the years, giving it a very broad scope.

When he defined what he called *the yoga of nutrition*, he spoke from experience, as in his fourteenth year he had discovered the true meaning of nutrition. Practicing this yoga had become natural to him. By endeavoring to eat his meals in a quiet and peaceful manner, he consciously transformed his food in "the laboratory of the mouth."

When he recommended nourishing oneself with light at the sunrise, it was because he had discovered the benefits of this practice when he was a teenager, prior to meeting Master Peter Deunov. He told us that when he was fifteen he would go every morning to the Sea Garden in Varna or to a neighboring hill to meditate and capture the first invigorating rays of the sun. And that remained so important for him throughout his life that, when travelling, he would ask for a hotel room from which he could see the sunrise.

> *When people begin to feel the need to nourish themselves with light and warmth, they will understand Creation and the meaning of life ... The divine world will open itself before their eyes and they will become sons and daughters of God. Everything is possible. Then they will distribute gold and precious stones to their fellow humans, who will also collect them from the sun, this untapped mine.*[3]

---

[3] Omraam Mikhaël Aïvanhov, lecture of July 18, 1964.

The intense spiritual life he advised us to develop, the meditations in the light, the spiritual work for humanity, all of this was natural to him. When he insisted on the importance of rising towards God, but also of working to bring Spirit onto Earth, he knew what he was talking about, for even though he was intensely spiritual, he was also very pragmatic.

It meant that he was capable of taking part in physical work with his brotherhood, of fixing things, as well as taking a great interest in the discoveries of our modern world. In the new technologies he found corresponding uses for our everyday life. He thought endlessly about how to make use of everything offered by Nature for the establishment of God's Kingdom on Earth. For instance, after learning about the new science of the laser at the 1967 World Fair in Montreal, he devised for his brotherhood a collective exercise to be practiced for the benefit of humanity: the creation, by the power of thought, of a spiritual laser.

What he said about purity, about the power of thought, about the importance of having a High Ideal, and about love, which, like the sun, organizes all life, reflected his own way of life. And yet, he never presented himself to his followers as an example. "Don't attach yourself to my person;" he used to say, "attach yourself to this Teaching. Go towards the sun, go towards the light." He also said: "We have been given the responsibility to put forth an absolute philosophy thanks to which one can rise to great heights … As for me, I am only a signpost! And what I am pointing you towards is the sun."

Another statement he often repeated along the years clearly shows his own detachment as well as the complete freedom he wished for us: "Don't take my word for it, go and verify what I say!"

Finally, while Omraam Mikhaël Aïvanhov remains for us an example of the marvelous philosophy of life he professed, it is his Teaching that can help us to transform ourselves … a Teaching of light, love, wisdom and truth.

Louise-Marie Frenette was born in Quebec. She studied Fine Arts in Montreal and Paris, worked for a number of years in an international association for humanitarian aid, and then taught Fine Arts. Later she began to write and publish books. The most important of these is the biography of Omraam Mikhaël Aïvanhov: *The Life of a Master in the West, Omraam Mikhaël Aïvanhov.* (Prosveta USA, and for the eBook, Amazon, Louise-Marie Frenette)

CHAPTER 1

Claude's Journey

"Ladies and gentlemen, we are beginning our descent towards the airport of Lyon Satolas. Please return to your seats, fasten your seat belts, and extinguish your cigarettes ... "

In 1976, I was working for Air France as a cabin crewmember. When making this announcement, little did I know that I was about to meet someone in this city who would change many things in my life ...

Some friends from Cambodia were hosting a party and had invited a few members of my family. Cambodia is the country where I grew up until the age of eight and a half. I wanted to join them, but the party was in Annecy, 145 km from Lyon.

Since I was supposed to spend the night in Lyon with the rest of the crew, I needed the authorization from the captain to go to Annecy. He didn't refuse, but warned me that being late would not be tolerated by our employer.

After calling to let my friends know I would be there, I rented a car and left for Annecy. My intent was to refrain from picking up hitchhikers. Having been one myself on many occasions, I often rendered this service, but this time I was in a hurry and decided not to. As I was about to exit Lyon, the traffic light turned green, and someone standing nearby caught my attention.

A young, smiling, blond man, all dressed in white, was hitchhiking. Reflex kicked in and I stopped, forgetting my resolution. I motioned the young fellow to join me and told him I was in a hurry, on my way to Annecy. He replied with a smile that Annecy was his destination as well.

I got back on the road, and soon we were engaged in a friendly conversation.

Looking at my white shirt, navy blue tie and the badge on my chest, he asked where I was working. "Up there with God," I replied, pointing a finger towards the sky. He didn't say anything, just laughed. Interestingly, he didn't pursue the matter and seemed to enjoy the image.

Why did I answer that way? I don't really know. He then began to talk about the upcoming Age of Aquarius and the changes that would occur ... about brotherhood on earth and about the love that transforms everything. It was beautiful and fascinating to listen to him.

Somehow, I had always felt a respect for "Heaven," so I listened intently to what my passenger was saying.

I wasn't involved in any religion or yoga practice, but I had always appreciated the spirituality of the American Indians and was quite open to the subject in general.

Our discussion was lively and engaging, our sharing sincere and interesting.

Dusk is that time of day when darkness begins to embrace the landscape, heralding the night. It was growing dark in the car, except for the dim, colorful glow of the dashboard lights.

My passenger took a tiny picture out of his pocket and showed it to me. I saw an extraordinary gaze, and immediately felt a warm expansion in my solar plexus. I looked ahead at the road again, but my eyes soon returned to the photo. I saw that this look belonged to a beautiful man with white hair and a white beard. Deeply moved, I asked who this person was. "Mikhaël" is all I remember him saying.

By the time we entered Annecy, the party had faded from my mind. At an underpass I stopped to let my passenger out, but that was not the end of it; we sat on the hood of the car and continued our conversation.

It wasn't until a few hours later that I suddenly remembered the purpose of my trip. It was one a.m.! He gave me a few brochures, and reluctantly we parted. I hurried off to the reunion of the old friends from Indochina.

When I got there the party was over, and everyone had assumed I had lost my way. I didn't explain otherwise, but went straight to bed, aware of my flight the next day and my mind still floating among the stars.

Months later, a friend picked me up to go play music at the house of one of his buddies. My friend described himself as "a mason who was working for a nice boss."

All went well and the energy was beautiful. At one point in the evening I asked for directions to the bathroom. It was located upstairs, accessible by way of a small orange room decorated with candles, pictures on the wall and a small altar ... with the very same picture of Mikhaël that the hitchhiker had showed me!

When I went back downstairs, my heart was pounding, and I told my friends about the trip to Annecy. They said I was now *in the net* and could no longer escape, and that I had to join them in the "Teaching of Mikhaël."

My friend hadn't dared to tell me who he really worked for. He had invented this story about working for a *nice boss*, who in fact was the Master Mikhaël.

The hitchhiker had shown me the photo of a being with an extraordinary gaze. Now, in the meditation room, I had found a picture of this same spiritual Master.

I have always believed that when we receive three consecutive signs, it is because something is important and worthy of attention.

I spent my childhood in a broken family. My father wasn't the tender type and eventually deserted us all. I was brought up by a very Catholic paternal grandmother and was sent to boarding school. My somewhat chaotic childhood clearly marked my behavior and my character.

3

Catholic boarding school left me with a sense of rage towards these men clothed in black, unmarried, and entrusted with my education.

Although I respected Jesus, I didn't appreciate going to mass three times a week. For me, this was nothing more than an opportunity to gather with some friends in the last row of the chapel for some silly fun and some snacks brought in by day students.

Out of curiosity, I read books like *The Third Eye* and the *Life and Teaching of the Masters of the Far East*. But what really interested me were the northern and southern Native American civilizations and their spirituality. I still have one of the books that moved me most: *Touch the Earth: A Self-Portrait of Indian Existence*[4]. I also believed that other civilizations existed throughout the universe.

I didn't enjoy going to church. It was only while in close contact with nature—mountains, forests, oceans—that I loved being with myself.

After that evening of music from the Andes with my friends, I joined the group of people who were following the teachings of this spiritual Master, Omraam Mikhaël Aïvanhov.

One day, when I was working as a volunteer on the property where the group held their summer gatherings, several of us were busy spreading guano fertilizer on future eggplant fields. A helicopter flown by a member of the group landed right in front of us, and the Master disembarked. He greeted us with a radiant face and the most beautiful smile in the world. The scent of roses replaced the smell of guano! My eyes were wet with tears, and I trembled with emotion. So the first time I saw this spiritual Master, he was *descending from Heaven*!

It would be a lie to say that my life was transformed overnight and that I became a saint. On the contrary, everything got worse. I didn't feel comfortable in my skin. Going from a meat diet to a vegetarian one caused my body to rebel. On top of that, I had to love everyone!!! It was a lot for a guy like me. But encountering

---

[4]   Teresa Carolyn McLuhan, Promontory, 1992, ISBN 978-0883940006

a spiritual Master teaches you something fundamental: that you are loved! In the face of that truth, those little problems faded.

From then on, the word *spirituality* took on a new meaning. With each gathering I attended and each of the Master's lectures I listened to, I was gradually becoming aware that I, too, was a son of God.

The Catholic religion had taught me that Jesus was the only Son of God, that we had sinned through Adam and Eve, and that many missionaries had become martyrs in Uganda and elsewhere in the world. Now a transformative change took place within me, even though I was not looking for anything in particular, neither a master nor an esoteric philosophy.

Unlike the priests of my childhood, the Master was always dressed in white. His beard was white and his hair was white. In short, everything about him inspired trust and a love for purity.

When we trust, we are open. Love, friendship, beauty, joy … all can come to us without meeting any resistance. Spirituality must have taken advantage of my openness to sneak in as well.

But despite it all, I chose ease and pleasure. What this Teaching required was still too arduous for me. I was not really ready to make sacrifices.

One of the fundamental ideas expressed in the Rig-Veda[5] is that all of creation, all life in the universe, can only come into existence through sacrifice. No creation or evolution is possible without it. Human beings can progress only through sacrifice. If this is demanding and entails great willpower, it also delivers tremendous results.

The methods recommended by the Teaching oblige us to overcome many bad habits, which is a form of sacrifice. In order for us to evolve, the Master sacrificed himself throughout his life, and that is an even greater form of sacrifice.

---

[5] The **Rig-Veda**: is an ancient Indian collection of **Vedic** Sanskrit hymns. It is one of the four canonical sacred texts of Hinduism known as the **Vedas**. **Rig means** "praise, shine", and **Veda means** "knowledge".

I had heard in one of the Master's talks that if you don't try to improve yourself, life will take care of that later on, but it will be more difficult for you. And more difficult it was!

But too often, in the midst of difficulties, we forget that life is teaching us a lesson: evil is only a misinterpretation of good.

What had I done to Heaven that made me have to face so many hardships? The answer was given to me by the Master: "Precisely because we have done nothing, or too little ... "
This signaled a profound need for change in my daily life.

To improve inwardly, we were asked to work with two principles: purity and harmony, for they pave the way to love. Love would then lead us forward on the path to wisdom. With some work, I would one day be able to bear witness to the truth of this process instead of just talking about it. How easy it seemed!

People talked to me about the concept of brotherhood, and the idea appealed to me. The only *small* issue was this matter of unconditional love for each other and for the world.

Once it is sowed, a seed germinates and grows into a plant according to its DNA. If it uses what the sun and Mother Nature provide, it will produce flowers, which in turn will become fruits. The seed will then have fulfilled its purpose.

Through these metaphors, I realized what the Master was telling me: that I too had a role to play and homework to turn in.

Then came the hardest part: to love myself in order to love others ... to love this bright region of my being where God dwells. I didn't know that the key to that region was hidden in my heart.

Some souls understand faster than others, because they have already undertaken this work in past incarnations. Others like myself understand, but only after lengthy explanations.

Well, what is important is to engage in this work, because it will lead us to what we all seek: happiness. Sooner or later, changes will occur within us.

I once heard the following idea: "God's greatest quality is patience." I know, you will tell me that all of God's qualities are great and perfect. Yes, but it is this sentence that helps me every day.

The yin-yang symbol has always intrigued me. In the black segment there is some white, and in the white segment there is some black. I like this oriental way of seeing things, in contrast to the perspective of Cartesianism[6], solely based on reason. Rationalism and unconditional love don't fare well together. When we apply this idea to our daily life, we discover that it contains a lesson in divine wisdom. Let me explain: we are sometimes faced with circumstances that disrupt our *daily peace*, and we equate these circumstances with trials and tribulations. Our instinctive reaction is to reject them and resent what is going on, without further reflection. Our immediate thoughts sound something like: "Why is this happening to me? This is so unfair!"

We normally forget that what happens to us is often a blessing in disguise, destined to improve us, an opportunity to turn a scar into a star. A change in our attitude helps us understand what is really happening. The challenges we face are only as drastic as our own degree of evolution, neither more nor less.

Initiatic Science[7] teaches us many great secrets. For example, when young children are learning to walk, they fall again and again, but they always get up and keep trying.

There is a scene in the movie *The Mission* that deeply affected me. The main character, Mendoza, a slave dealer played by Robert De Niro, arrives in a South American indigenous village carrying a heavy bundle over his shoulder containing his armor and sword, a self-imposed penance for having killed his brother in a fit of anger. One of the village warriors, following his chief's orders, rushes to Mendoza, grabs him by the hair, puts a dagger to his throat intending to kill him. But instead, he cuts the rope

---

[6] Cartesianism is the name given to the philosophical and scientific system of René Descartes and its subsequent development by other seventeenth century thinkers, most notably Nicolas Malebranche and Baruch Spinoza.

[7] It is the science based on the laws of the cosmos and on nature which all Initiates and great Masters study, verify and transmit to their disciples, thus the term *Initiatic Science*

to his bundle, thus releasing Mendoza from his burden. The indigenous warrior has forgiven the Spaniard who came to invade and conquer his country, to sell him as a slave in order to grow richer! I wept when I saw this scene. Only later did I realize the value of its message: I saw myself dragging along this heavy and useless burden that was my past ... I had to let go of it if I wanted to enter the world of light.

Why do some sentences speak to us more than others? Consider this popular one for instance: "To be, or not to be." Everyone knows it, but many prefer: "To have, or not to have." This is a good illustration of how we often fail to grasp the truths the Initiates reveal to us.

To choose this path of evolution is far from easy, but it has one special quality: it gives us the opportunity to experience different points of view and to meet people of quality.

Little by little, I saw my life becoming more beautiful. Was it actually becoming more beautiful, or was I simply beginning to see it in a different way?

This inner journey is required if we want to bring our shadow side into the light.

The ego is very vigilant, like a good sentry, constantly on the lookout for the slightest thought and gesture to serve its own interests. It has a fantastic weapon: time, and it knows how to use it. We can always hear our ego expressing itself, but the little voice of intuition is there too, advising us, speaking softly ... alas, often too softly!

Finally, everything boils down to a question of trust and faith. Ever since I put my trust in God, my life has had a better flow. My prayers are those of gratitude instead of requests. Healthier food keeps me free of disease; conscious breathing sustains my health; and as for my love for Heaven, I keep it alive everyday with a very short but powerful prayer: "Thank you." I also use this prayer in the most difficult moments, because I know that my message will be heard.

Coming back to my relationship with spirituality, there are traps to avoid. I can tell you about it, because I have fallen into them, like Obelix who fell into the cauldron of magic potion when he was little.

Being engaged in a spiritual teaching will not spare us from having to resolve our karmic debts, and being a spiritualist will not protect us from major events. Most importantly, let's not speculate about being saved or belonging to an elite. We are subject to whatever life presents to us, be it easy or difficult.

During a trip to India, I learned that when something happens to us, in itself it is neutral, neither good nor bad. What matters is how we react to what is happening. Too often we mistakenly allow our emotions to control our reactions. Sages of the past spoke of *maya*, a term meaning that what exists on Earth is but illusion.

Attempting to step back from life events isn't easy, but it opens up a pathway to compassion and love.

I appreciate the following tale from the Native Cherokee: "Two wolves battle within us, one black and one white," said a father to his son. The son asked: "How do we know which one is acting in us?" His father answered: "It depends on which one you feed ... " The black wolf represents our ego, whereas the white one represents the bright space within us, home to our divine spark.

We can only awaken to spirituality through selflessness. This is where the famous *unconditional love* takes the stage. Restated again and again in so many poems and songs, unconditional love is a selfless love, with no hidden agenda. It is a love made up of gratitude, faith, joy, forgiveness and compassion; it has the purity of a ray of sunshine and the power to make angels smile.

The experience of unconditional love is not always a given, because we have a past, both in this life and in previous ones. This love dwells within us but is buried under many layers. And remember, the key to it rests in the depths of our heart.

An extraordinary woman became the embodiment of unconditional love: Mother Teresa. Those who have wandered the streets of Calcutta will understand me. To be able to hug beggars and very old poor people, to give them what they are most deprived of—love, consideration, comforting and food—is such a demonstration of unconditional love. I understood from this what one of the greatest prophets of our history once said: "Whatever you do to the least of these little ones, so you do unto me." Spirituality began to make sense to me.

When we decide to enter the world of light, the door doesn't open immediately. We have to rid ourselves of many burdens, and this is the biggest challenge. We have to offer a sacrifice of sorts, and show Heaven our true interests and efforts.

Here is a story I love: on his way to the ashram of his guru, a disciple hears someone calling for help. As he approaches a well, he realizes that the voice is coming from the bottom of it. He leans over the edge and extends his arm to a man struggling in the water below. The disciple shouts: "Give me your hand!" But the poor fellow does not react. After shouting the same thing several times, he realizes the man is drowning. Indeed, he soon disappears, as death carries him off. Upset, the disciple runs to the ashram and his guru, who asks him what happened. The disciple tells the story to his master who wants to know every detail. "What did you shout to him?" he asked. I said "Give me your hand!" Yes, it was good of you to want to save him, said the guru, but you see, it would have been better to say, "TAKE my hand".

I thank my Master ... he is the one who told us this story.

Claude Brun's biography:

Born in France, I lived in Cambodia from the ages of six-and-a-half months to eight years old. I lived in France, Germany and other countries for work until I settled in Canada in the 1990s.

I have worked in publishing and in the airline industry. I was self-employed in construction and have been a researcher.

Now that I am retired, my main interests are: organic gardening, playing music, photography and working with the light.

Claude wrote the chapter on Melchizedek in our first book.

CHAPTER 2

Sally's Journey

It is hard to say how it happened, how I became aware of the spiritual aspect of life. But it happened. It probably started with someone giving me a copy of *The Prophet* by Kahlil Gibran, and then another friend sending me to a dance therapist in West Los Angeles who did work you didn't talk about; it was something you did. From there, it was probably following visits to the Bodhi Tree, a beloved bookstore for the "in" people that offered mysterious and other-worldly books, as well as a wide range of philosophical and spiritual literature.

It was a time when young people drank herbal teas and ate huge salads at health food cafes on the Sunset Strip or Melrose Avenue. It was the time of HAIR, The Beatles and the influx of mind-altering drugs.

At that time, there were a lot of alternative influences, but it was one particular dance therapist who sent me in a direction that changed my life dramatically.

I was very thin as a young woman, so thin that while doing this free-form dance work, I was unable to sit or move on the floor; it was too painful, as my bones protruded awkwardly. The very wise dance therapist sent me off to meet the most extraordinary people I had ever met: Dr. Giovanni Boni and his wife Therese.

Giovanni Boni was an acupuncturist and homeopathic doctor practicing at home under a chiropractic license. At that time his name was secretly passed from one person to another to insure his safety, as he was operating somewhat outside the law. Acupuncture was forbidden in those days, and the general understanding was that it was used in the Orient to simply block pain and nothing more. The American Medical Association was highly suspicious of anyone who claimed to be an acupuncturist.

Gianni's office was filled with unusual items: beautiful stones and crystals, small pyramids, symbols carved in wood, and images of interesting people from faraway lands. There was also a window through which the sunlight always seemed to shine, no matter the time of day.

Gianni began treating me with needles and prescribing various homeopathic remedies. Slowly I improved, but I was still rail thin. He cleared areas in my consciousness that allowed beneficial and prophetic dreams to flow through.

Gianni's wife, Teresa, was equally fascinating and had her own business in their home teaching languages. She had discovered and developed a unique method of learning languages involving movement. She taught her methods to many people who came to her home studio every week. Some days it would be French, some days Spanish, and there was even some dabbling in Russian. Everyone loved her. She was dynamic, dramatic, magnetic and stunningly beautiful. She was a great cook and welcomed anyone who wanted to be in their home. I was one of them. I was lucky.

I was enchanted by these people and wanted to be around them all the time. I can't remember exactly how I was making a living at the time. I think I was still working in Beverly Hills running Paul Simon's music publishing company, Charing Cross. In any case, my work stopped shortly after getting to know the Bonis.

Therese began asking about my life and discovered that I had been a tennis champion. She used to claim I had won

Wimbledon, but actually I had only won the junior division there and had been a semi-finalist in the Women's Division. It was useless to try to put her straight about this, but she put me straight about a lot of things: she got me right out on the tennis court to teach, and even became my first student. Through the dance work and the Zen philosophy I had been studying, I ended up creating a way of playing tennis that was entirely different from the tennis I had been taught. It was all about moving from the inside, in a natural, un-programmed way. I found it was the most fun you could have on a tennis court. My style of teaching led me to private courts in Beverly Hills and Malibu for several years, teaching stars like Joel Gray, Larry Hagman, Jill St. John, Helen Reddy, Milos Forman and Barbra Streisand, to name a few. The funny thing was that my method of teaching tennis had elements that were very similar to the language method Therese had created.

During those early times with the Bonis, I was led to read the books about Joan Grant's past lives, the Zen books of Hagel and Alan Watts, Elizabeth Haich's beautiful *Initiation*, and books about Ramana Maharshi and other saints.

Their home seemed to be a magnet for extraordinary and spiritually inclined people, and I became a fixture there, a fly on the wall, absorbing everything that went on. It included visits from the highly respected astrologers from Sedona, the tremendously gifted Sufi Richard Field from England, the yoga erudite Georg Feuerstein, their friend Kathryn, who was a renowned clairvoyant, and a number of other fascinating and enlightened people. But greatest of all at that time was the opportunity to be in the presence of Michael Malachek, a swami and spiritual Master who had been in the caves of Arunachala with the great one, Ramana Maharshi. Michael was a musical genius and had played a dominant role in the sound track of the 1940 film *Fantasia*. He was already in his eighties when I met him. At that time he still walked two miles a day, played the cello, ate pure food and did his most important work at night. I later found out that there are only four people like him on earth at any given time, and that he was not here as a teacher, but to help maintain harmony on this planet. He was, of course, highly evolved and very powerful to be able to do this work. To be in his presence was a great gift and one that made me feel I was connected to more than the ordinary life that most people lived. Also, in his presence you dared not speak of anything that was not absolutely true or spiritually correct, or he would set you straight immediately.

Michael's eyes were as blue as the sky on a clear day, and they could look right through you. Therese called Michael the Master of Purity. We all learned from him the value of maintaining the physical body in its purest state. "You have to keep the glass of the lamp clean so that the light may shine through," he would say.

The first time the Bonis' took me to visit Michael I had a short, private consultation with him in which he asked me the ultimate question: "Do you will to do good?" I answered, "Yes." It was a kind of initiation. I've often thought of that statement and what it means. It is quite a life-changing declaration that affects everything you do and all the choices you make from then on. It is so simple, yet infinitely meaningful.

Well, even with my intention to do *good*, my choices were not always spot on. I bounced around, from this to that, trying to maintain balance. It seemed my history of extremism would always get the best of me; that is, until Gianni pointed it out.

I had taken meditation to new heights, entering states of consciousness that I had no support for. Falling into a Kundalini experience, I ended up in a trance, will-less and motionless for days on end. Again, Therese and Gianni came to my rescue and nursed me back to health, or I would have ended up in an asylum.

During my recovery in their home, Gianni asked me one day what I thought my Achilles heel was. I had no idea. "Extremism," he said bluntly. Well, yes, now that he pointed it out, it made sense. I was raised as a champion, and it was tennis, tennis, and tennis. Years before, when my mother took me to Dr. Bieler to set up a proper athlete's diet, he said I needed to purify my system first, and zucchini was the recommendation. So that's all I ate: zucchini, zucchini, zucchini. No wonder I got so thin. When I began writing little inspirational books, I wrote one every day. When I fell in love with teaching tennis, I taught 8-10 hours a day. When I fell in love with men – well, never mind.

So "balance" became my new mantra. Balance in food, work and rest, and ok ... men. What a concept! The middle road is a very safe place to be, and perhaps the wisest. Therese used to quote one of the great ones (it may have been Hermes Trismegistus) with a line that went something like this: "Life should be approached as if you were walking a tightrope above a deep crevice." This implies how treacherous life is and how important wise choices are.

I took what I had learned from my time with Gianni and Therese and went back into everyday life, "calling in" my man. I had learned a few tricks that I used to create what I wanted in my life, and it was time for "my man" to be a part of it.

Not surprisingly, this ideal man showed up on a tennis court. One of the places I taught my special brand of tennis was on the court of Jennings Lang, one of the top executives at Universal Studios. Jennings was a generous, loving man who was always supportive of my art. Unbeknownst to me, he intended to set me up with a very influential man from Hallmark.

Marv Huss, then head of advertising and promotion for Hallmark Cards, had flown in from Kansas City to purchase a property, *The Snow Goose,* owned by Universal. He wanted it for the Hallmark Hall of Fame television series. Jennings was in charge of making the deal, and in doing so he insisted that Marv stay through the weekend and sign all the papers on Monday. Fortunately, Marv had brought along his tennis racket, and Jennings suggested he join the fun on his court Saturday morning. As I was a part of the tennis socials with Jennings, I was told to bring a portfolio of my artwork along with my tennis racket.

When tennis began, that good-looking Midwesterner was across the net from me, and above him an enormous blue light flooded the sky. Oh, I thought, I'm supposed to pay attention to this person.

After a few sets of tennis, we were on the sidelines looking through my portfolio. It was all a bit esoteric for "Mr. Hallmark", but he was gracious and attentive. I later learned that he was always being set up to look at someone's art. In any case, he was kind to me.

I had planned to continue playing more tennis that day in Malibu, so I invited Marv to join me. After tennis, our day became ... a walk on the beach, lunch at Alice's on the pier, dinner in Brentwood and then dancing in Beverly Hills.

I was hooked. But it took two years for Marv to sort out his life and make room for me. In the meantime, I played a few tournaments for fun and ended up on the Virginia Slims tour, which took me through Denver where Marv had moved to open his own advertising agency. There, we planned our future.

Our first step together was operating a small tennis club in Ormond Beach, Florida, then a large club in Aspen, Colorado, which we developed for a businessman out of New York. It was there that our son Michael was born.

After a few years in Aspen, we wanted to return to sunny California. That's when I again made contact with Therese and Gianni Boni. I had one foot in touch with their spiritual activities and the other one rooted in my personal and family life. It was at that point that I learned of the Master Omraam Mikhaël Aïvanhov. As I was a busy wife and mother, I only had one ear open to the spiritual realm.

One afternoon, Therese Boni brought me up to speed by telling me how she and Gianni had discovered this Master and his work. They were still living in California and had flown to Paris on their way to Italy for some event. On their ride into the city, Gianni, a great collector of books, wanted to visit his favorite bookstore before going to their hotel. He went to the second floor, but Therese was tired and stayed on the first floor. Her eye caught a brightly colored cover of a small paperback. It was one of the books from the Izvor Collection by Omraam Mikhaël Aïvanhov. She opened it, read the first paragraph and knew this was a Master. Despite her fatigue, she ran upstairs and found that Gianni had the very same book in his hand!

From then on, the Bonis became acquainted with the books, the Teaching, and the Master himself. They eventually started a study group in Los Angeles to gather like-minded people and introduce them to this Teaching. Later on, the Bonis and their friends brought Master Aïvanhov to California.

They had organized a way to import the books so that those who were interested in the Teaching had access to the many books already published. Therese had told me on many occasions that it was the Master's desire that the focus be on the distribution of the books. Therese had even set up a promotional campaign and created appropriate advertisements for bookstores, encouraging them to carry the books. Naturally, The Bodhi Tree was one of the stores delighted to put the Master's books on their shelves. They even offered the use of their lecture hall for Therese and Gianni to speak about the Teaching.

It was during one of the Master's visits to California that Therese encouraged me to come to one of his lectures, which was to be held in a large auditorium in Santa Monica. The place was packed. All I remember about the evening was the effect his presence had on me. I was in awe; my third eye was pulsing. The audience was attentive and respectful.

Two days later, I had an appointment with Gianni. He laughed here and there as he spoke of that evening. He could see what we could not. He said that one of his patients complained that the Master kept repeating himself. Gianni, who was clairvoyant, said that this patient was not aware that there were endless higher beings on another level working on the individuals in the audience, and that the Master had to hold the audience there until the work was done.

I went to other smaller gatherings, one held in the living room of a devotee. I was late and wandered in with another friend. Oh, the reprimand we received was something I will never forget! A stern, penetrating look and a few short words were all that were needed to humble me. How could I be so thoughtless toward one so worthy? From then on, I would make sure I would arrive well in advance, even if I had to get there the night before.

Another gathering I attended was in the home of the Bonis. Therese and her friend, the wonderful musical genius Rachel, had prepared their group for the Master's visit by learning several of the Brotherhood songs in Bulgarian. After he arrived and was seated, they sang to him. He was so moved that he had to leave the room for a few moments, deeply touched by this genuine offering. Those were the only times I was in the Master's presence. I wish now there had been more of them.

Through the years, I have gathered quite a collection of the Master's books and have delved into them, sometimes continuously and sometimes sporadically. There is not one paragraph that does not ring true to me; I keep finding information that is always useful. Each thought is something to digest and live by.

The Bonis eventually moved back to Italy, and Therese's group in California scattered. Gianni passed away and was buried in his beloved Italy, but Therese would still return to Los Angeles once a year to visit her dentist and her dear friends. On each of these occasions, I would find a way to spend time with her.

Every gathering Theresa created would consist of a few close friends sitting attentively around a dining table, while she went over one of the Master's lectures. Then, she would speak extemporaneously about the theme. It was on those occasions that she shared wonderful anecdotes about her time with the Master. Therese had travelled with him, as a kind of interpreter and personal secretary and assistant, while he lectured in cities across the U.S. and elsewhere. She told us how surprised several of his followers had been in New York when the Master had charged for one of his lectures. This had never happened; he had always spoken free of charge. After this event however, he gave Therese the money that had been collected. It was quite a sizable amount. He told her to put it away and that one day she would know what to do with it. Therese forgot about the money until she was assisting Georg Feuerstein to prepare to write a biography of the Master (*The Mystery of Light*). It was just the amount of money needed to pay for the project!

The Master also had a great sense of humor. Therese would tell one story after another, which revealed his delight with life. One day while in France, Therese was washing Rachel's hair in a little sink in their room near the Master's accommodations. While walking nearby, he stuck his head in the door and saw the washing going on, and then for the rest of the day described it to everyone as Therese trying to drown Rachel, laughing wholeheartedly every time he told the story.

Like many great Masters, he was also very strict. Once, he really let Therese have it. He was extremely angry with her about something, the details of which I have forgotten. She left his cottage quite shaken. On her walk back to her room, she ran into one of the "sisters" who was staying at the Bonfin and who asked her what had happened. Therese told her, and the sister replied that the Master must truly love her; he would never have reprimanded her in such a harsh way unless he deeply cared. Therese felt relieved.

I also remember a story she used to tell about a time when the Master was in Los Angeles and they were preparing for a gathering. Therese, who was flamboyant in many ways, wore one of her more exotic outfits. The Master was appalled and criticized her for the brashness of her dress. Then he softened and said that if it really made her happy to wear that outfit, he didn't wish to dampen her joy. In that case, she did not need to change. I found it so interesting that he valued her joy over his sense of what was appropriate.

So much of what I learned about the Master I learned second-hand through the wonderful people I have been so blessed to know. One of the things I heard was that the Master indicated that the spread of this Teaching in the U.S. would have to start in California. Therese was doing the promotions for the books, and fortunately an amazing woman came forward at this time to handle all of the importing and distribution of the books in the United States. Prior to this, several of Therese's friends handled this on a volunteer basis.

Wanting to help Therese find more outlets for the books, my friend Evelyn and I had the idea that Dr. Wayne Dyer would be just the right person to speak about the Master and his books. I tracked down Dr. Dyer's contact person who explained that the only way to speak with him was to go to one of his lectures and catch him at a break. That was enough for Evelyn and me to pack a bag and head for his next lecture, scheduled in San Francisco. The place was packed. At the first break, we charged forward amongst many others hoping to have a few personal words with Dr. Dyer. We were lucky and managed to speak to him briefly with great enthusiasm. He listened very carefully and responded: "Send some of the books to my home in Hawaii."

The books were sent with the hope that he too would be inspired by the Master's wisdom.

A few years later, my husband was watching Dr. Dyer on one of his PBS seminars. I was not present, but Marv reported to me later that day, "I saw Wayne Dyer on a PBS special, and he mentioned something about his new teacher Omraam Mikhaël Aïvanhov!" This was so exciting that I immediately went to the Internet, did a search on YouTube and found the seminar in which he indeed mentioned the Master!

I called Susan Rashkin, the loyal and generous woman who had taken up the task of handling the distribution of the Master's books in the U.S., and told her that Wayne Dyer had mentioned the Master on a PBS special. She laughed and said that only a couple of weeks before she had spoken loudly to the Universe, saying: "Why can't we have someone famous speak about Master Omraam?"

Inspired, I immediately wrote to Dr. Dyer by post, and on the envelope I wrote: "About Omraam Mikhaël Aïvanhov." My idea was to get him as much information as possible on the Master and also to put him in touch with people who could shed important light on him and his Teachings. I received a thank you package from him with some of his books, CDs and a letter. It said, "I loved your letter. I love Master Omraam as well as his teacher, Peter Deunov. Thank you so kindly. I am called to make his spirit known. Sending you love, Wayne."

Later, when I saw that he mentioned Omraam Mikhaël Aïvanhov in his book *Wishes Fulfilled,* I was thrilled. With this mention both in the book and on PBS, I felt it was a sign, perhaps a starting point for the diffusion of more light from this great Master, this great teacher. The feeling that something was happening with the Teaching on a grander scale warmed me.

At the time, I was still working on my art and design projects and putting all of my licensed products in signature galleries around the country. However, the climate changed, and no matter how hard I worked, the economy was against me. My galleries, which were really "happy stores," began closing, one after the other.

I was down to my last gallery, in La Jolla, California, and was running it myself when a friend stopped in for a visit. Jan and her husband Ian, both motivational speakers, took me out to dinner. We wandered down to the La Valencia Hotel for a little music. We were about to sit down when Jan noticed Jack Canfield and his wife Inga on the dance floor. "Come and meet Jack," she said. Jack, of the *Chicken Soup* books, was considered "the guru of success," and Jan had worked with him for years, assisting at many of his seminars.

After a bit of small talk, Jan insisted that the Canfields mosey down for a look at my gallery, which was open late. Jack looked around and asked, "What do people say when they come in here?" "That it's bright and happy," I replied, "and that it feels good to be here." Jack shook his head in agreement.

Then Jan and Ian entertained Inga so I could have some private time with Jack. He looked around some more and then began telling me about some of his spiritual experiences. He revealed that a great "seer" with whom he was often in contact had told him that he was supposed to be working with *The White Brotherhood*[8]. This was the opening I had hoped for.

I immediately handed him the large pictorial book called Omraam Mikhaël Aïvanhov, created to mark the 100th anniversary of the Master's birth. "This is the man you want to know," I said proudly.

Jack sat down at our counter and looked intensely at every picture, reading every line underneath it. When he seemed satisfied, he put the book down graciously and said to the others. "We can go now. I have found what I was looking for."

Again, I had hoped somebody important would be willing to open a great conversation about this wonderful Teaching and this great Master. I, like Therese and so many others, had only to read a few lines by the Master to know the depth of the truths he was giving us. I had a feeling that the same thing had happened to Jack.

Not too long after that first encounter, my friend Jan insisted that I attend one of Jack's weeklong popular *Chicken Soup* seminars. She went to great lengths to get me to one being held in Scottsdale, Arizona.

I had a moment or two with Jack alone over a rushed luncheon. I had had the sense that all these highly popular motivational

---

[8] Keep in mind that "white" in this instance refers to the purity of the soul and not to skin color or ethnicity. The White Brotherhood is an invisible organization comprising all the great Masters, Saints, Seers and Prophets who work for the advancement of mankind.

"stars", these transformational leaders, spoke in a similar language. It was as if they would gather together, decide what the new theme to promote would be, and then go out to their followers and pass on the information via books and lectures in words consistent with those of the others. Interestingly, after being in this group seminar with Jack Canfield, I found it to be true. The main inspirational spiritual speakers of our times actually do go to some exotic destination once a year and discuss the subjects they feel are important for people to understand.

Well, I thought of suggesting to Jack one of the subjects the Master considered of highest priority, described in the book *Spiritual Galvanoplasty*[9]. In this amazing book, the Master explains how every pregnant mother can consciously prepare herself to influence for the best the formation of the child in her womb. There is another wonderful book on this subject as well, entitled *Education Begins Before Birth.*[10] I had even spoken with John Assaraf, one of the contributors to *The Secret,* about spiritual galvanoplasty and the importance of shedding some light on this process. I eventually wrote a tiny pamphlet on the subject called *The Golden Child Method,* about bringing in "good kids", and referred to Master Aïvanhov's book in the hope that the reader would want further information on the mother's role in forming and educating her unborn child.

Anyway, I told Jack about Spiritual Galvanoplasty and said that the information came from *The White Brotherhood.* He listened to me and said I should send him this book. I did. I was so hoping that someone like him could open the door for more of the Teaching to be spread.

At the end of the weeklong seminar with Jack, he took all 250 participants through a wonderful guided meditation in which we walked through a meadow and then climbed a spectacular mountain. Atop the mountain a beautiful golden angel appeared,

---

[9]   Omraam Mikhaël Aïvanhov, Izvor collection #214, Prosveta S.A.
[10] id. #203, Prosveta S.A.

holding a gold box. She opened the box and to each of us revealed our "life purpose". Whew! Who wouldn't want to know that?

When that golden angel removed the lid from the golden box, out poured my life purpose: books, endless books. They fell down on me in a stream. I was to write books! Naturally, that's all I had secretly wanted to do, but had never done. I was always trying to make enough money to have time to do just that. So I went away from this most wonderful seminar, ready to start my new career.

Master Omraam often emphasized that we were to spread the Teaching through his books. It wasn't only about gathering in groups (although this is important too), but getting the books into the hands of people who in turn could better themselves and their lives by working in a very practical way with the principles and truths he revealed. He spoke for over forty years, and all of his lectures were recorded so that his Teaching could be preserved and available to scores of readers. Collections of his lectures are now preserved in a great number of books on every subject anyone could want to study.

Surprisingly, the Master did come to me in a dream around this time and thanked me for what we did for "the Brotherhood." I thought it was very revealing that he said, "*for* the Brotherhood," and not for himself. It was never about him. He came to enlighten humanity. Of course!

I know these beautiful books are now in many hands, as they have been translated into more than 30 languages and are distributed and sold all over the world. But my deep hope is that they will be in *more hands* in the United States. With so much propaganda of fear that the newspapers, Internet and social media pump out every day, these books are a welcome relief, offering plenty of hope, inspiration and wisdom. But I often wonder: "Do people really want wisdom today? Does it sound old fashioned?"

Much earlier on, I had been tempted to run off to India and seek enlightenment, or follow the latest, greatest, fashionable guru. When I met the Bonis, I knew they knew this about me. I always trusted there was someone who knew what I needed to know, even when I wasn't aware of it.

After studying the Master's books, it made sense to me that the Indian way was not my way or the best way for a Westerner. I was definitely not destined to be a spiritual yogi, but to be a regular person with certain talents that could be used to benefit others. It also made sense to me that we are all here to do some "good" in a practical way, not to escape this world into nirvana.

I saw the disasters so many experienced by neglecting the business of their everyday life and following a so-called spiritual leader. Long ago, during conversations at the Bonis', I learned that there would be many false prophets showing up. Unfortunately, there are probably still more to come. My friend Mary Ann almost lost herself by following a false Sufi. My friend Carmen from California nearly lost her fortune to a false mystic from India who amassed 74 Rolls-Royces from the purses of his worshippers! How many others, hoping to find a higher purpose, were led down the garden path, only to find out that it led them to a dead end ... or left them without much money in their wallet! Our Master teaches us about discernment. What a skill this is to acquire!

The information in his books is practical and useful on a daily basis. We no longer need to go off to some ashram to be tested; the testing can take place every day, wherever we are. We can develop ourselves and improve our lives thanks to our inner work. Master Omraam gives exercises, techniques and examples to help anyone who wishes to go higher and, in the process, brighten the lives of others. Major concepts are offered for contemplation with proof of their truth: the idea of reincarnation; the importance of understanding hierarchy; the realization that our work in the present will influence our future. We are also taught the value of giving thanks at all times; the acknowledgment of a living nature; the awareness of our indebtedness to our parents and country, to nature and the universe. These are just a few examples of subjects the Master covers so thoroughly.

For many years I have created a syndicated column for newspapers (King Features Syndicate[11]). It is called *Happy Musings* and consists of short, inspirational thoughts, which I also illustrate. They appear daily in newspapers and are designed to shed a bit of light-hearted perspective on readers' lives.

Long ago, Therese was browsing through a list of my musings and came across one that caused her to hesitate. It stated: "Make your goals crystal clear, and surely they will become crystallized." She said: "This is not quite true. You are dealing with the Truth in what you do, and it must be accurate."

As she suggested, I changed the line to read: "Make your goals crystal clear, and surely they will become crystallized, provided life doesn't have something better in mind." That satisfied her. And it is true: so often we want what we want, when really we should want what we need. Life knows best.

Therese was a tremendous influence in my life, as she was in the lives of many others. Her great presence was magnetic and inspiring. She filled a room just by herself. She passed away in 2013. I will always love her, miss her and see her in the light.

Many of the themes of my children's books reveal truths from Omraam's teachings, which are alive and embedded within me.

Now, after all my years of twists and turns and experiences (I am in my seventies at the time of this writing), I have settled down to do the work the *golden angel* revealed to me long ago. I write and illustrate my children's books to my heart's content. Kindle Direct Publishing and Amazon have made it possible for me to create the books I have dreamed of and to make them available to a wide audience.

From having a good attitude (*Attitude is Everything!*), to being appreciative (*Did You Ever Say 'Thank You'?*), to being cooperative (*Getting Along with Each Other*), to being kind and helpful (*The Princess in my Teacup*), to following your heart (*The Little Leprechaun Who Loved Yellow*), to valuing a mother's love

---

[11] http://kingfeatures.com/about-us/about-king-features-syndicate/

(*Who took my Banana?*) and more, there is a lesson inside each of my books, now numbering eighty. I feel I am one of the lucky ones who was introduced years ago to this amazing teacher, Omraam Mikhaël Aïvanhov. I have had time to work and live with his Teaching and have found myself better for having done so.

When I look back, I am often in awe of the many people who have passed through my life and offered me ways to stay in "the light." But of them all, none has ever touched me as deeply as this great Master, through the wisdom in his books.

Life is wonderful!

Sally Huss's biography:

From a very young age, I was fascinated by children's books and delighted by their illustrations and whimsical rhymes. As I developed my own art skills, I felt a desire to write and illustrate books for children myself.

Although I did many others things in my life—becoming a tennis champion; working in films for Samuel Goldwyn, Jr.; running Paul Simon's music publishing company; developing a successful art career with 26 Sally Huss Galleries across the country—I have finally returned to my heart's desire.

Presently, I write and illustrate books for children that will uplift their lives by passing on essential values, as well as subtly encouraging the development of emotional and social skills, and all the while tickling their funny bones.

I am grateful for the teachings of Omraam Mikhaël Aïvanhov, which influence my life and work daily.

CHAPTER 3

Mark's Journey

Letter to my sons:

Dear Jasper and Blue,

You are my beautiful boys, and it is because I care for you so very much that I am writing you this letter. As your father, it now feels important to let you know who I was before you came into my life. I want to share with you a part of my story, but more importantly, I want you to know my values and some of my beliefs.

My Early Years

I was interested in pretty much all the things you are interested in now at your current ages of 12 and 10. I was a happy guy, had lots of friends and really enjoyed life. I also remember the delight I felt when I made people laugh and saw that they were happy. You may feel the same way now. I feel you both have inherited this joy of life from me.

I was always excited about learning new things and thinking about my future adventures. You have heard me tell stories of my childhood and teenage years at the dinner table or during car rides. I told you about my little adventures at the age of 10 when

I crossed the frozen North Saskatchewan River in the winter to go tobogganing at Little Red River Park, or when I was playing music in a band, or was paid to break-dance in a night club at the age of 14. These memories are all great, but I would especially like you to remember my story just after I finished high school.

Venturing Out

When I was 18 years old, I moved away from the small town of Nipawin, Saskatchewan. I had saved over a thousand dollars and was ready to spread my wings. I wanted to live in the big city of Edmonton, Alberta, which was eight hours away by car. I took a bus because it was a slower way to travel and gave me lots of time to imagine what I would do in my future. I felt like I was on my first big adventure!

Reality strikes fast sometimes and it did so when I looked around at the people on the bus and saw that a lot of them looked unhappy. I wondered if this would be the same in the city. All the exciting ideas I had contemplated while on the bus sustained me for a while, but I lasted only three months in the big city. I was homesick. The experience did open my eyes to a lot of things I had not experienced in a small town, like the crazy traffic, the endless commute to and from work, and all the people! I knew there was something better out there for me and I wasn't going to find it in Edmonton. Strange, even though I was homesick, I didn't want to go home. I still needed an adventure! So I packed my bags and went to live with my older brother Garth, my sister-in-law Tammy and their newborn baby girl in Prince Albert, Saskatchewan.

You are brothers, and it may seem now that when you are older there would be no way in the world you would live together. But living with my big brother Garth and his family gave me a sense of pride and fulfillment. During my short time with them, I had a chance to bond with my little niece, your cousin Chantelle, who is now 27, and we had a wonderful time all together. The best memories are when Garth and I would get out our guitars and play our favorite songs well into the night.

After only a few months of living with my brother, the opportunity came for me to move to a resort in the Rocky Mountains and work as a waiter in a big fancy hotel chain. I took this job in a heartbeat and still clearly remember the drive into the Rocky Mountains. Leaving the foothills just outside of Calgary, the snow-capped mountains became visible in the distance, and as we approached them, the sight of these giants made me almost explode with excitement. It was the same feeling I had experienced when I was just 8 years old and my parents and I drove through those same mountains on our way to British Columbia to see my grandmother. I wouldn't take my face off the car window for fear I would miss seeing another magnificent peak. The smell of the mountain air was amazing! To me, it is sweet, and you can even taste it! To this day it is still my favourite scent. They say that the Rocky Mountains are some of the oldest mountains on the planet.

When I arrived at the resort it was dusk and the mountains where towering around me. I felt at peace. I felt at home. This was exactly where I was meant to be at that time. I was taken for a tour of the grounds. We looked over an immense valley. The stars and moon helped to light up the mountain above us. It was Mount Kidd, the most beautiful mountain I had ever seen. Beautiful, shimmering snow lit up its huge, sheer face. I just couldn't comprehend the size of these mountains compared to anything I had ever seen. Remember, I was from the prairies, the very flat prairies! The wind came up from the valley, pushing me backwards, yet I knew I was going forward in a most wonderful way, and felt like the luckiest man alive.

Being a waiter at this resort was great. As both of you already know, I have a happy disposition, and working taught me how to truly serve others. In time, this job led to an opportunity at another resort in the Rocky Mountains called Panorama. I spent a season there and learned to downhill ski on my days off. Then

I was off to British Columbia, Penticton, for the summer and Big White for the winter, and then, on the cusp of my 21st birthday, I made Vancouver my home. What an adventure I lived during those few but so influential years of my life!

Self Discovery

It was during this time in Vancouver that your father's life made a big and fantastic change. I was working as a bartender at a small pub near Kitsilano Beach in Vancouver. A waiter named Robin would often be on the same shift with me. We had great ease in talking to each other, and our conversations were very interesting and uplifting. Needless to say, we became friends.

One night after a shift, we went for a bite to eat. I can still remember this evening, as the conversation I had with him was life changing. He shared with me that he was part of a spiritual group and that he followed the philosophy of a spiritual Master, an Initiate. I had never heard of someone referred to as a spiritual Master or an Initiate. I had so many questions! As you know, I am very curious by nature. I was so intrigued with Robin and what he was revealing to me. That evening he told me he would bring me a book that would introduce me to this Master's teaching.

The pocket book he gave me was *Man's Two Natures, Human and Divine*[12] by Omraam Mikhaël Aïvanhov. After reading the first chapter, I knew something was about to change. What I had just read touched something so deep and vast inside me, almost as if it had struck an inner tuning fork that had been dormant until that moment. All of my uncertainty in life seemed to disappear, and the words were completely in tune with everything I had always believed in. I could feel myself nodding as I read through those first pages; it all seemed so right, so wise, so loving and kind. The chapter introduced the idea of man's two natures: one, which is lower and selfish, and the other,

---

[12] Izvor Collection, #213, published by Prosveta S.A.

which is kind and divine. That night, August 19 of 1990, I wrote in my journal: "I will develop many traits of character that will bring me closer my higher nature." I was hooked.

It wasn't long until I had read the entire book, and I couldn't wait to read more, learn more. I awoke every morning with a burning desire to become a better person and to attune to my *higher Self.*

A few weeks after reading the first book, I attended a meeting where others who followed the teaching of Omraam Mikhaël Aïvanhov gathered. It was there that I was introduced to the organization which refers to itself as the *Universal White Brotherhood.* We meditated, ate a meal in silence and listened to a lecture by Master Omraam, recorded in France back in the 1980s. Even though he was Bulgarian, the Master spoke in French, and someone at the meeting translated his words into English for me. I felt very comfortable in the ambiance created by the others, referred to as brothers and sisters, who gathered to hear his wise words.

I have always been attracted to sacred spaces such as cathedrals and churches, so being in silence, listening to beautiful sacred music and a fantastic lecture was perfect for me. The people I met there seemed buoyant and vivacious and looked straight into my eyes with sincerity and kindness. Once again, just as I had felt in the mountains, I was home, but this time it was my spiritual home.

Living the Teaching

From that point on, I focused my life on learning more about the Teaching and working on myself: on my thoughts, my feelings and my actions.

I applied the Teaching in all aspects of my life. It had a distinct and incredible effect on my inner happiness and peace of mind. I learned about meditation, breathing exercises, fasting, eating, health, colors, sexual energy, pregnancy and prayer. Learning from this Teaching seemed endless!

After more than 25 years, I still begin each day placing consciously my right foot on the floor when getting out of bed, saying:

'Thank you God for this new day.' I also always wash my face and hands before starting my day, leaving behind the fluidic impurities and welcoming fresh energies.

How many wonderful experiences in my life I attribute to the teaching of Omraam Mikhaël Aïvanhov! His influence has helped me make sound choices. He showed me the way to a high ideal that I have nurtured and continue to nurture.

A New Business

Shortly after, I became roommates with Claude, a brother from the Teaching. He became a true and wonderful friend. We spent a lot of time playing music, talking philosophy, and he helped me start my first business, selling beeswax candles. Not only was the idea of selling a beautiful, natural product attractive to me, but the idea of spreading light around the world also seemed ideal. I was introduced to the business through other brothers living in Toronto who would sell me the candles, which I, in turn, would sell to stores on the West Coast. That wonderful business created for me a good income and a great lifestyle.

Meeting Your Mother

Claude and I decided to take a summer off, venturing out to play music at festivals and promoting the books of Master Omraam Mikhaël Aïvanhov. It was an extremely memorable experience, as we would perform everywhere: from a beach on the Pacific Ocean, to the towns of the Rocky Mountains, to the front of an old post office in the Prairies.

It was during this most memorable trip that I met your mother, Francine. Claude and I had performed just in front of her booth, where she was selling jewellery she had crafted herself. Claude was on the lookout for me, as he knew I wanted to find a life partner. Later that day he said, 'I found the girl for you!' and pointed in your mother's direction. I remembered playing in front of her booth and noticing her beauty. I walked over, introduced myself and put out my hand to shake hers. To this day, I remember Omraam's words explaining that you can tell a lot about a person by how they shake your hand: whether it is too strong, too limp, or just right. Your mother's hand fit most beautifully into mine ... a natural fit. A few months later your mother and I connected again in Vancouver, and we have been together ever since. I was 23 years old and she was 22.

Your Birth

Before either of you was born, your mother and I understood the importance of creating a child. We wanted the best conditions for each of you to come into this world. We waited about ten years before deciding to have children, until our relationship and especially our love for one another had grown strong.

The philosophy of the teaching of Omraam Mikhaël Aïvanhov explains that the mother has the power to attract all the best elements of health for the child she carries in her womb. Through her thoughts and emotions she attracts a soul corresponding to the inner conditions she creates. We were both very conscious during your gestation and constantly prayed for beautiful, kind, loving and generous human beings to be a part of our lives. You are the result of your mother's conscious work, and both of you are wonderful boys. Your names were also very important to us, as a name carries a certain vibration and power. We wanted each of you to have not only a name with a nice sound but one that conveyed a feeling of strength and creativity. We are so happy we named you Jasper and Blue.

Why we are Vegetarian

You may wonder why we are raising you boys vegetarian. I also know it may be difficult at times for you to explain why you are vegetarian. You have told me that sometimes you have felt different from others at school and haven't known what to answer when questioned about it. I am sorry if this has caused some stress in your young lives. I know we have given you a few simple answers, like we prefer not to kill animals, but I would like to tell you why I chose to be vegetarian.

The first time your mother and I went out to dinner, I told her right away that I was a vegetarian. She lit up, as she had just become a vegetarian two weeks before that. She said I was the first vegetarian she had ever met and was so happy we had this in common!

Just one week after being introduced to the teaching of Master Omraam, I had decided to become vegetarian. He gives a number of different reasons why the vegetarian diet is ideal, but the point that struck a chord with me was when he explained:

> *When animals are about to be slaughtered they sense what is about to happen, and they are terrified. This terror causes them to secrete toxic substances, and there is no way of eliminating that poison from the meat. Thus, when man ingests meat it is not conducive to good health or long life.*[13]

In my experience, being vegetarian made me more conscious of what I put in my body and how it reflected on my behavior and my health. All animals fear for their life, which can breed aggression. It is known that vegetarians tend to be more peaceful, compassionate and respectful. You will see later in life

---

[13] Omraam Mikhaël Aïvanhov, *The Yoga of Nutrition*, Izvor Collection, # 204, Prosveta, U.S.A. 1991, p. 57

how the choice of being vegetarian adds building blocks to your health and vitality, and how it sharpens your mind. When you eat food that contains the most direct energy from the sun such as fruits, grains and vegetables, you strengthen your physical, emotional, mental and other subtle bodies.

Watching the sun rise

You have seen me out on the deck in the morning, facing the sun. Have you ever wondered what I am doing? I am working with the sun. A very important aspect of the teaching of Omraam Mikhaël Aïvanhov is to attend sunrise from the spring equinox to the fall equinox. The sun is a reservoir of light, which can fill us not only with physical warmth and energy but also with spiritual light. Moreover, it is the physical representation of God and of selfless giving. Master Omraam taught that *"the closer we get to the sun in spirit, soul and thought, heart and will, the closer we come to God, for, on the physical plane, the sun is the symbol and the tangible, visible representative of the Deity."*[14]

Gratitude

Every day I am so very grateful for the life I have, for your beautiful mother and for you, my strong and kind sons. If there is one thing I feel is absolutely important for both of you boys to practice, it is gratitude, contentment. In the face of great sorrow and strife, this will be your saving grace. Even to be thankful for your trials, as trials can make you stronger.

Kindness

I keep talking to you about kindness, but are you aware that your kindness can create for you a promising future, that you

---

[14] Omraam Mikhaël Aïvanhov, *A New Earth, Methods, Exercises, Formulas and prayers.* Complete Works, Vol. 13, Prosveta S.A., 1988, p. 146.

have some control over your destiny and future? I live by the law of Cause and Effect. What you put into life, you will get out of life. So look for kindness and live by the motto: 'It is better to be kind than right.'

Love and Light

'*Love and Light*': for many years, you have seen me write cards or emails ending with *Love and Light*. You may know what *Love* refers to, but perhaps you don't know what *Light* stands for.

> *Light is the subtlest state of matter, and, conversely, matter itself is no more than light in its most condensed form. The whole universe therefore is made out of the same matter ... or the same light ... condensed or subtle, to a greater or lesser degree. Everything that you find condensed on earth exists on the etheric plane in a finer, purer form. The whole point of our spiritual work is to learn how to find what we need in a higher, finer, more subtle state, so that we can once again draw near to our original state.[15]*

When you send light to others through your thoughts and written words, you are spreading the subtlest form of God. You are helping others to find the source of life; you are emanating the highest form of love.

What I wish for in the future

Through the teaching I have been following and the different businesses I have created, I came to realize that, for me, the most important thing in life is the ability to serve others. I

---

[15] Omraam Mikhaël Aïvanhov, *Light is a living Spirit*, Izvor Collection #212, Prosveta S.A. 1984, p. 21

Awakening: our soul journeys

hope the work I do on myself, as well as my achievements and successes, lead me to help and coach both of you and others, both in businesses and other life endeavours. At the end of this lifetime, I want to be able to look back and say: "Thank you Lord, I have served to my best, and my boys have learned from me."

Jasper and Blue, through this letter you realise I have found a path that gives me a reason for going forward and appreciating life. It is my sincere hope that through our example, your mother and I have instilled in you a foundation to live by so that you both enjoy a bright future!

Love and Light,

Dad

Mark Walker's biography

I currently live with my wife Francine and two sons, Jasper and Blue, in Kelowna, British Columbia, Canada. I am the owner of a Vacation Property Business, which specializes in Summer Vacation Homes in the Okanagan Valley and Ski Resorts throughout British Columbia. I started this business in 2003 and currently employ 10 people. With a passion for travel and adventure, I have taken a number of trips to Nepal during my leisure time, and I enjoy exploring the outdoors, skiing; hiking and sailing. I love to spontaneously jump in the car and get away with my family to the mountains as much as possible.

Visit my website at: www.OVHR.com
Mark wrote the chapter on Economy in our first book.

CHAPTER 4

Carmen's Journey

My youth

Born to a family of six, I was the third girl to see the light of day. We grew up happily as an ordinary family. My father worked hard at selling and repairing household appliances from our back veranda. With time, he built a store at the corner of a main street in Joliette, Québec. With his natural ability to connect with people, he was able to develop a trustworthy relationship with his clients and became successful. My mother, a great support to his business, took care of the paperwork while attending to the needs of all the rest of us: four girls and two boys.

As the business grew more prosperous, my parents were able to invest in a cottage by a nearby lake where we spent our summers swimming, water skiing and exploring the area.

Already at a young age, the paranormal beckoned me. At the cottage one summer when I was seven years old, I told my dad that in my mind's eye I saw the motor falling off our boat, just before it actually happened! My dad somehow retrieved the motor by the gas cable and we rowed back home. I rushed to my bedroom to cry under the blankets, not because the motor had fallen off, but because of the image that registered in my mind before the incident happened. It scared me, as I somehow believed that it was I who had made it happen. Somewhere deep within I already knew that thoughts were powerful. It is known that some young children bring psychic abilities with them from the "other side', but because most parents or teachers do not respond, they are often misunderstood, mocked, bullied or rebuked. These children eventually block the flow of their extrasensory perceptions. A new book has just been released on this subject entitled *Memories from Heaven: children's astounding recollections of the time before they came to Earth*[16] which confirms this point of view. In my case, I kept asking questions, many questions, which most of the time remained unanswered.

Going to church every Sunday was engrained in family traditions in Quebec at the time. One day, I said to my mom, "Why should I go to church just because everybody else goes? Why can't I just stay home, but be a good girl all week? I promise to make my bed every day, I'll do the dusting, anything you ask, but I don't want to go to church just out of habit." My mom answered: "Why are you so different from the others? Really, where do you come from? Come on, put on your hat, take your nickel and get going." I was rather upfront with my feelings, so much so that at times I was considered rebellious. It is not that I didn't believe in God; on the contrary, I remember during my primary school years inventing little songs I would sing to God, thinking of myself as the 'fool of God.' I would skip down the street coming back from school, singing spontaneously to myself. It never occurred to me to share the songs with anyone. It was *my* inner world and mine alone. This secret and sacred space with its little songs brought me tremendous joy. It was a way to connect with God, and even though I may not have liked going to church every week out of habit, I had nothing against Him. Something sprang forth from within me that I did not hold back!

Only in hindsight did I realize that I had inherited part of that ability to connect to the divine from my mom's fervent faith (who, as I type this text, is still praying at the respectful age

---

[16] by Wayne Dyer and Dee Garnes, Hay House, 2015, ISBN-13: 978-1401948528

of 96) and also, I suppose, as part of my own inheritance from previous soul journeys on Earth. Much later on, I took time to write my mom to tell her it was the best gene she had given me: her love for God! Although not very sentimental, she said that reading my letter brought tears to her eyes.

When I was born, my parents thought I should eventually become a nun (they apparently nearly called me Carmelite). Didn't every good Catholic family have to have a nun or priest amongst their children? One day when I was about eight years old, my father brought back beautiful photos of "air stewardesses" from one of his overseas trips. I would stare at those photos for hours. At one point, tugging at my mom's dress, I told her: "Mom, going to Heaven is hardly reachable for me, but going into the sky, that is possible!" Considering that I was the 'naughty one' amongst my siblings, becoming a nun didn't seem to fit my style, but flying in the sky was a real calling. From that day forward I knew what I wanted to do when I grew up, and I never changed my mind.

In the following years, as my father travelled abroad, he kept taking more photos of flight attendants, and I collected them. Meanwhile, I began reading interesting books that also captivated me: *The Third Eye* by T. Lobsang Rampa[17] and *The search for Bridey Murphy* by Morey Bernstein[18]. The latter spoke about reincarnation, which fascinated me. I was almost 14 years old and had to hide these books under my mattress so my parents wouldn't confiscate them or report me to the priest. They still kept an eye on me!

It was evident that if I wanted to keep my dream alive of becoming a flight attendant, I would have to learn the English language. So I asked my parents to send me to an English school. They finally agreed to my incessant requests. At the age of 16, I

---

[17] first published by <u>Secker & Warburg</u> in 1956 and republished on several occasions.
[18] first published by Hutchinson, London, in 1956 with a film adaptation produced by Paramount.

was registered in an English boarding school in Rawdon for the last two years of my secondary schooling.

It was during those two years at boarding school that I experienced something rather disturbing: it was as if something in my brain would tie in a knot, and a tremendous pressure would build up, causing me to faint. This occurred from time to time through the years, until one day the explanation stared me in the face: while reading the life of some saints, I learned that until their energy was channelled into a spiritual life, they suffered some form of neurosis or psychic disturbance. Indeed, once I woke up spiritually, these symptoms disappeared.

After attending the English school in Rawdon, I went to O'Sullivan College in Montreal and graduated as a legal secretary. I began working for a lawyer in the city for a year or so, waiting to reach the age of majority at 20 when I could apply to the airline. Meantime, the Government of Canada changed the age of majority to 18. I was so excited, I wrote to all the airlines I could find in the telephone book. I had my first interview with Air Canada, and when the lady asked me my purpose in becoming a flight attendant, I answered that I wanted to travel, that I wanted to go to Tibet and didn't know if I would come back! Well ... as you can imagine, that didn't go so well! Meanwhile, my roommate Serena invited me to travel the world with her for a year. She worked for a cargo shipping company, and we would have a free trip to England. I had my passport ready, and one week before our departure, Nordair called me for an interview. I was now 19 and I refrained from stating the same purpose as before. I simply said I wanted to travel, see the world and would rather be paid to do so. That did it. I was hired.

Flying around the world

A few weeks into my probationary period, I was called for a flight to Resolute Bay in the Arctic Circle. It was August, and we landed in a beautiful, perpetual sunset. There were no trees and the land was flat, but it appeared like a shallow bowl with pink snow all around. It was magnificent. I asked if I could go for a walk. I put on the company parka and boots given on the Arctic flights and deplaned through the stairs. I literally walked out on the runway and just kept going into that pink glow. There was such a sensation of infinity and freedom that I became mesmerized. Suddenly, I heard a siren. When I turned around, our aircraft appeared so small in the distance! I ran back and begged the crew not to report me. Of course, knowing I was newly hired, they laughed at my enthusiasm and accepted my venture, as long as I promised not to do that again. I didn't know then, but a thirst for space and infinity was calling me. Much later I learned in the initiatic school that each of our different bodies requires a specific form of nourishment: the body needs food, the mind feeds on light, the heart on love, the soul on space and the spirit on eternity. Unconsciously in that experience, my soul had been fed by that sensation of infinity.

The routes Nordair was flying soon bored me. I longed for more diversity and wanted to see the world. So I applied to Canadian Pacific Airlines whose network covered a number of continents: Europe, South America, Asia, and the Pacific. I was hired immediately. Great opportunities to see many places in the world now opened up to me. I was meeting so many interesting people on flights and during layovers. I also admit that, together with other crewmembers, we enjoyed the good life while discovering the best restaurants and visiting the different cities during our stopovers, even though changing time zones ended up affecting my sleep.

One day, my roommates and I were approached by a young man close to where we lived who had befriended us and who eventually suggested that we bring drugs into Canada. We outright refused and never saw him again. Another time, during a vacation in the Greek islands, I met the owner of a cruise liner who unexpectedly flew to Montreal a few months later and called my mother, asked for permission to marry me and offered her all kinds of rich promises. I was not in the least bit interested and had told him so before, but now I had to make it clear to my dear mom that I certainly would not marry him just because he was rich! Another time, however, one of the flight attendants and I entertained the idea of becoming "accompanying hostesses" to business men in the city, for dinners and shows. We talked and laughed about it but never actually followed through with it. It seemed there was always an angel at my side protecting me from choices that could have been devastating. Opportunities grew like branches on a tree with options to follow any one of them, but somehow I stayed close to the trunk and just kept looking up!

A turning point in my awareness came when I was traveling with my roommate Susan. We were in Egypt, returning from the Great Pyramid of Giza, traveling via the desert road back to Alexandria, when our bus broke down in the middle of the night. We were told we had to wait until morning for a mechanic or another bus to meet us, and were advised not to go out of the bus because of snakes and scorpions. Hours went by. To entertain ourselves, Susan and I looked through the window at the stars: there were gazillions of them! We began to ask each other questions such as: Why are we born in a certain country and not another? Why are we here on earth? What is the purpose of existence? Are we the only ones in this infinite space? Had we been influenced by the energy of the pyramid that day? Or was it the vastness of the desert? These existential questions were to follow me home. It seemed a new window had opened in my consciousness, and now I wanted a clearer vista. I really wanted answers to my questions so I could better understand life. Why was I born in Canada and not in Egypt where people were all wrapped up in dark clothing in such heat, and plowing their fields without eating all day long (it was Ramadan, that time of the year when Muslims fast from dawn to sunset). Who decides where one is born? Is there justice in the system of birth and death? I was overflowing with questions. Why was I feeling such an avid thirst for more meaning in my life? Why was this thirst so insatiable, despite the great living conditions I already enjoyed? Why, why, why? I recognize today that in wanting to understand life better, it was knowledge of myself I was looking for, knowledge of my Self, the divine nature within me.

In 1975, the airline reduced the flight attendant base in Montreal, and several of us were given the choice to remain on a lay-off status or to exercise our seniority rights by moving either to Toronto or Vancouver. I was ready for a change, so I moved to our headquarters in Vancouver. The flying was not so good for the junior flight attendants, with many night flights across the country. With such a schedule, making friends was not easy, committing to any activity was nearly impossible, and eating and sleeping irregularly was playing havoc with my body. Although I was doing what I had always dreamed of, something inside was missing. I needed to anchor myself better and find some balance in life. So I registered for a Hatha yoga class, remembering that my friend Jacqueline had told me years earlier that ever since she had practiced yoga, her life was in harmony. That awakened something in me.

My yoga years

Fall was approaching in Vancouver, and I was missing the colorful scenery in the East. As my vacation was scheduled for October and the Hatha yoga suited me, I remembered that Jacqueline had also mentioned a yoga school in Vermont. I thought this would be a great location, with autumn foliage exploding with color, but how was I to find that school? I had not been in touch with Jacqueline for years, and there was no internet in those days.

During a layover at a Montreal hotel, something moved me to look into the city's Yellow Pages. It didn't really make sense to find a Vermont yoga school in a Montreal phone book, but I just kept looking, pushed by an intuition or by shear stubbornness, the later often having served me well in life! To my surprise, I discovered an ad for the Yogi Inn in Vermont, connected to a yoga class on St Denis Street in Montreal. I called the Vermont center and was told that a one-year program had just begun, and that I was welcome to join in during my vacation as long as I agreed to be part of the group's activities and didn't expect a one-on-one teaching. The price was reasonable, so I confirmed my arrival for early October.

The person who opened the door to the center when I arrived on a Friday evening was none other than my friend Jacqueline! Isn't that amazing? She too couldn't believe I was the guest who had called from Vancouver wanting to come for three weeks. What a coincidence for both of us. But are there really such things as coincidences, or is it a superior degree of awareness? Unconsciously, maybe both our souls were calling for something more in life, and we would finally get answers to our many questions.

My spiritual life takes flight

During the first week at the yoga school, I thought for sure the eighteen people attending the yearly program must all be depressed or suffering from some kind of ailment. I couldn't believe that anyone could go through such a disciplined routine for an entire year unless they wanted to become a yoga teacher, or unless something was really wrong with them. I attended the three yoga classes a day but kept falling asleep during the fifteen-minute relaxation at the end of each class. Jet lag was catching up with me. Meditation sessions were held morning and night. I discovered that my mind was the wildest, noisiest horse one could ever imagine; or I would literally fall asleep sitting up! Needless to say, I was not attracted to the meditation classes at that point, so I skipped them after a few attempts. The activity of the day I liked most was the morning reading. The whole group would sit in a circle while our yoga teacher read a chapter a day from an inspiring book. Afterwards, we were free to ask questions or discuss the subject. The book the group was reading upon my arrival was *The Life and Teaching of the Masters of the Far East* by Baird T Spalding[19]. I knew nothing about spiritual masters, so I was intrigued by this book and never missed a morning.

During the third week, I began to realize that the people there were not as bizarre as I had originally thought. They were inquisitive about a part of themselves they had tapped into by reading books or attending other yoga classes and wanted to deepen their self-discovery. I too began feeling as if little windows were opening within me. I gave meditation another chance and finally stopped falling asleep. With the help of controlled breathing, I was beginning to tame this wild horse of mine. I was receiving answers to questions I had had since childhood. As I thought it was too soon to go, I extended my stay another week.

After that one-month vacation, I returned to Vancouver and resumed my flying schedule, but my mind kept retreating to the yoga school. What I had discovered was definitely not taught in any standard schools. I asked for a one-year leave of absence, but to my disappointment, my request was denied. I said, "OK, I quit," and that was it. I knew without hesitation that I had to go back to the school. I had lived twenty-four years to find myself precisely at this juncture in life.

Looking back, I believe a very supportive guardian angel had protected me step by step, leading me to this crossroad. I was so thankful. Finally a new meaning was given to my life, a conscious meaning, a conscious awakening. Yes, I was climbing a tree, and if I had managed to avoid a lot of unsafe branches, this time I was not going to miss such an opportunity to grow more wisely and consciously. I was so grateful to be finding some answers ... and they were finally quenching the thirst within me. Moreover, I was sleeping and eating regularly, not drinking any alcohol, and feeling healthier and happier than ever before.

---

[19] Self-published by himself in 1924 and later republished by DeVorss, USA.

So I quit the airlines and moved all my belongings back to my mother's place in Montreal. She was horrified: quitting my job, selling my car and going to live in a yoga school ... in the United States! She really thought I had lost the plot!

It was early December by the time I arrived permanently at the Yogi Inn. It was nice to reconnect with everyone and get back into a discipline of well-being. Some of the exercises our teacher Gérard Fortier invited us to practice was testing our intuition on our own, one hour a day. For example, we had to take a deck of playing cards, sense what color the top card was and record how many we got right. Another exercise involved holding a pendulum over the cards, asking out loud if the card was red or black and counting the number of times we were right. We were also taught how to use the heat coming from our hands to make a paper fan turn. Basically, we had to observe ourselves, distinguish between our intuition and our ego, and try to work from intuition as much as possible.

Our day began at 6 a.m. with a swim in the pool, then a roll in the snow and another swim in the pool. This was followed by the hatha yoga class, respiration and meditation, breakfast, a reading session, individual intuition practice, more hatha yoga, respiration, meditation and lunch followed by a two hour break. Then a kundalini yoga class, hatha yoga, respiration, meditation, dinner followed by a short break, and finally at the end of the day, we were to write in our diary. In our writing we were asked to comment on the feelings that surfaced in our daily routines. Days and hours went by fast, and I was never bored. Once in a while we would watch an inspiring movie on a Friday night. And once a month a weekend of activities was created for outside guests, and we were free to join them if we wanted to. These were our only distractions during the year.

When I returned, the group was reading a book about *Man's Two Natures: Human and Divine*[20], or in other terms, the lower

---

[20] Omraam Mikhaël Aïvanhov, Izvor collection #213, Prosveta, ISBN 978-2-85566-326-5

self and the higher Self. One of the students told me she knew about the author, Master Omraam Mikhaël Aïvanhov, and invited me to look at some of his other books. When I saw his photo on the first page, I was mesmerized by his wise regard, his serene gaze, and I said to my friend, "I wish I could meet him one day." She told me he was a living Master and that in fact the book we had read earlier, *The Masters of the Far East,* was a bit far-fetched and not a true account of what Masters really are. That left me a bit perplexed, as I had no frame of reference whatsoever for how spiritual Masters lived.

During that year at the yoga school, I experienced some pretty incredible states of being. For example, my senses and thought process became so acute that I would think: "I'm cold, it would be nice if someone closed the window", and at that exact moment, someone would get up and close a window. Another time, I would think: "It would be nice if someone called me", and a few minutes later, *ring, ring*: "Carmen, a call for you"! Had the thought come from me or from the doer? If I had sensed in my youth that the mind was powerful, I was now discovering that this was only the tip of the iceberg!

One day, our yoga teacher, who was also an acupuncture practitioner, was showing us the meridian system and invited anyone who wanted to be treated to come forward. Some who wore glasses went up, others with minor ailments went up as well, but I stayed quietly behind. At the end, he looked around and found me: "Come here, I've got something for you." He put the needles in specific places on my head and face, then told me neither to move for a few minutes nor to ask any questions. When he removed the needles I was in such a state, it was incredible. In fact, it was shear elation! The grin on my face made everybody laugh. I didn't have one negative thought! I even tested my own state of being after dinner. I went outside to the back of the building where a pile of junk had accumulated which I always thought was a real eye sore. It was on the path leading to the trails in the forest where I loved to go during breaks. To my surprise, I couldn't find anything negative about the pile of junk. My only reflection was that every household needed a place to stow their unneeded articles. How amazing that I could even come up with such a solution! That night I didn't want to go to sleep for fear of losing that magical state. Sadly, it was gone the next morning. Noticing my reaction, Mr. Fortier called me to his office and asked: "How did you like that state of mind yesterday? Know that if you work on yourself, you can reach that state of bliss yourself. All I did was stimulate your pineal gland by positioning the needles accordingly. We all hold within ourselves the potential of divine states of being. It's up to each of us to work inwardly and earn them."

It was also during the year at the yoga school that I experienced out of body travel, or astral travel. It was not part of the exercise program, but I supposed it was a result of the regular discipline we practiced and the pure life we lived. While I was lying in bed one night, my consciousness lifted above my body. I was not sleeping; on the contrary, I was in an acute state of awareness. I saw the face of Mr. Fortier, who was waiting for me. More than ever I realized that we are not just a body; we are a soul, and we can direct our awareness to different regions. I experienced such a state on several other occasions, although I don't encourage anyone to develop it without the guidance of a pure and disinterested spiritual guide, for the invisible realms are also inhabited by undesirable beings with ill-intent.

The year's program was coming to an end, and it was time to think of what I would do next. I didn't want to go back to the airline because of the crazy lifestyle, the irregular sleeping and eating patterns, and so on. I wanted to teach yoga, but could I earn a living that way? Just before leaving the Yogi Inn, Mr. Fortier told me that I would go back to the airline. I asked him: "What makes you think I will go back?" To which he answered: "It will be the best way to measure yourself." Well, that went in one ear and out the other. I didn't really understand what he meant, and I was NOT going back to the airline.

September arrived, and it was time to say our goodbyes and part. What a year it had been! I returned to Montreal and stayed at my mom's place for awhile until I found my direction. I had to earn a living. A yoga studio in Montreal was looking for a yoga teacher for asthmatic children, so I applied and was accepted, but the job was only once a week. I worked as a waitress in a restaurant briefly until one of the patronages offered me the position as receptionist at his real estate development company across the street. I accepted immediately and moved into the area with some roommates. I kept my hatha yoga practice and meditation going but found it really hard to have a social life. I didn't want to go back to my previous lifestyle and friends, so I began to read one spiritual book after another to fill the void.

About ten months after leaving the yoga school, a friend from Vancouver called saying that Canadian Pacific Air was looking for part time flight attendants for the summer. I had realized that I really didn't like working nine to five. I couldn't survive on teaching yoga alone and thought it would be nice to travel again for just three months. After completing the necessary steps, I was re-hired for the Montreal base. During those three months, I noticed how much my attitude had changed. I was more stable in my activities, had more patience with passengers and was able to handle the irregularities of my schedule without as much stress as before. When autumn came, the manager offered me a permanent position. Unfortunately, I had just registered for a course in metaphysics in the United States for all of November. He asked what I wanted most: the airline or the course? I thought for a moment and said, "Well, really, I want both." He didn't know what to make of me … He thought for a minute and finally said: "What if we give you a leave of absence for November and you come back after that?" That was perfect! Would you believe that I am still flying now some 40 years later? But with metal wings … I am still waiting for the more subtle ones to grow …

On a mission

Just as I hadn't believed that being a Catholic was the only way to God, I didn't believe yoga was the only way either. I was on a mission to prove to myself that several paths lead to God. As a matter of fact, I sometimes didn't even want to pronounce the word God. He had acquired some pretty negative publicity through the hostilities amongst various religions and even within the same ones! So I found myself referring to God as the Supreme Energy or the All Being.

Like a butterfly, I "gleaned" from one school of thought to another: Eckankar, Rosicrucian, Cosmic Science, Unity School, etc. For a couple of years, I attended many self-development lectures and participated in many seminars. After a while, I felt I wasn't growing in depth and was rather scattered from running from one system to another, yet I recognized that they shared a common sense of truths, as if there were a universal link between them. So, I decided to stop everything and draw within to find a direction. For sure, I could not be the only one on Earth thinking and feeling the way I did. There had to be other people on the same wavelength, believing in such "different" things such as reincarnation and vegetarianism (I had been a vegetarian for several years) and I wanted to follow that universal track and find my spiritual family, but how? So, I put a note under my pillow that read: "I want to find my spiritual family based on nothing less than Universal Love and Cosmic Light." I prayed every night by my bed, down on my knees, repeating my affirmation.

Some months later my friend Jacqueline, whom I had not seen much since the yoga years, moved closer to Montreal and invited me to a concert of the Evera[21] choir she had just joined, which I gladly accepted. Something interesting happened during the concert: in the midst of their singing I felt a fountain rising in my chest and flowing over me as tears. They sang in a language

---

[21] The Evera choir had two parts to their concert: profane and sacred. The sacred songs consist of a series composed by Master Peter Deunov, meant to elevate the soul through their content, meaning and purpose.

I didn't know, so it couldn't have been the words. I remembered my yoga teacher saying: "Truth ... you cannot analyze it, you feel it". After the evening, I asked Jacqueline to get me another ticket for their next concert. I needed to better understand my reaction to their singing.

A few months went by and, while attending another one of their concerts, I again felt the same sensation, with tears pearling down my cheeks. This time, two words they sang stayed with me: "Jivot blagen, Jivot blagen." For several days, those words would follow my every thought. I called Jacqueline to ask her what it meant: "Blissful life," she said and invited me to join the choir practices in Montreal, some fifty km from where I lived. I said, "No thank you, I don't feel like making any effort at this time in my life," to which she answered: "Wait until you are suffering, then you will really have to make efforts!" And she hung up. She is an irresistible friend, the kind of friend who isn't afraid to share her truth, whether one likes it or not. Some forty years later, we are still good friends. In the unfolding of our paths, she always seems to be a step ahead, inspiring me onward.

To come back to her comment, although I had decided to stop my gleaning, I concluded that she might have a point: it was better to make efforts while the going was easy than being forced to make them while in pain, because then, not only would I have to deal with the pain, but the efforts as well. So I went to the choir practice the following week. It was a tough decision, because as a young girl I had been dismissed from the singing class in school. The nun told me I had no voice! So joining a chorus was surmounting a real stumbling block. The singing director was most encouraging and told me that if I could speak, I could sing. He tested my voice and concluded I was a soprano. Their repertoire was mostly in Bulgarian, so I was learning Slavic words with an English accent in a French Canadian community, and that got me a few glances! But while attending practices, I learned that the other members of the choir were also vegetarians, and all were students of the teaching of Omraam Mikhaël Aïvanhov, the Master with the beautiful, serene gaze I had seen in a book at the yoga school some four years earlier. How interesting!

As I had read about the *Dark night of the soul*[22], a state of consciousness in which the ego resists any form of evolution or connection with God because it knows it will lose ground, I was determined not to fall into that phase of resistance, so I gave myself one full year before evaluating my commitment to the chorus and deciding whether or not to quit.

I also began reading the books by Omraam Mikhaël Aïvanhov and attending the Sunday meetings in Montreal where the choir practices were held. The books were not actually written by Omraam himself. His numerous lectures were audio or video recorded and then transcribed into collections of books. It is said that there are enough lectures to fill 500 books.

About four or five months into the singing practice I felt like quitting and had all kinds of excuses: flying and singing schedules were difficult to work out, the extra traveling time back and forth between the airport and meeting place, and so on. Nevertheless, I associated that resistance to the *dark night of the soul* and persevered through that phase in order to keep my promise not to quit for the full year. I also faced a wall of resistance when I attempted to go to the first "intergroup" meeting of the "Brotherhood"[23] in Laval. The first time, I got lost on the way and never made it. The second time, my old car broke down, had to be towed and was beyond repair. On the third attempt, I remember standing by the door before leaving my house, looking up to Heaven and saying out loud: "Nothing, but absolutely nothing, will stop me from making it to the Brotherhood meeting today; do you hear me?" And I finally made it. I had won a battle with my ego!

---

[22] St John of the Cross, first published in 1584 and now available through Dover Publications.

[23] The "Brotherhood" is an association of brothers and sisters who practice the methods taught by Master Omraam Mikhaël Aïvanhov.

It was not much longer after this episode that I recognized that the people with whom I was spending several hours a week shared many of the beliefs I had held since childhood or had later welcomed into my life. They felt like my "brothers and sisters." I had walked through a *dark night of the soul* and at last had found my family of souls! They were all stable people, working and attending to their family's obligations. During these early times of getting to know my "soul family," I found myself smiling inwardly or even weeping with joy during our rehearsals and concerts. I even started to sing by myself in the car, with that same unbounded enthusiasm I had had as a young girl. My consciousness was elevated to a new state; it was a Golden Age! I knew without a doubt that as the one-year commitment would come up on the calendar, I wouldn't hesitate to continue walking this new path.

Meeting a Spiritual Master

The following year, in 1981, I went to *Le Bonfin* for the first time. It is the international center where people from all over the world gather during congresses at specific times of the year to practice the methods taught by Omraam Mikhaël Aïvanhov. It is located on the Riviera in the South of France in a locality called "Bonfin" which means "good ending". It was September, and I managed to get a whole month off to truly "feel" my new family. It was beyond any expectation. I was living Heaven on Earth and was bathed in such a harmonious ambiance that tears rolled down my cheeks every day for the entire month. Sometimes it was the wonderful singing that uplifted me to realms I had never experienced before. At other times, it was the Master's words during his talks that overwhelmed me to tears, or it was watching the beautiful dance of the paneurythmy[24]. I thought surely only angels could dance like that!

Le Bonfin is a special place where the spiritual atmosphere is so sacred and respectful that little windows open up inside one's consciousness, little awakenings which in turn bring serendipities. For example, one day I was invited to breakfast at a sister's place where I met an older brother. He told me that for many years he had been a Buddhist monk living in Tibet. His spiritual guide eventually told him to go back to his native land, because he had taught him everything he could, and that he would meet his next teacher in the South of France, all dressed in white. This brother inquired about my coming to the Teaching, and I told him about the fountain effect I had experienced when I first heard the songs, and how I was still so moved when singing in the Great Hall. He said it is because the songs remind us of our soul's lost paradise. My throat was tight with emotion. In that single meeting I had received answers to two of my questions: one concerning my connection with Tibet and the fact that I didn't need to go there anymore, and the other regarding the songs and why they had such an effect on me. I also learned by going to the singing practices that these mystical songs had been composed to illuminate the mind, warm the heart or stimulate the willpower. They have a tremendous harmonizing effect, both on oneself and on the collective consciousness as well.

One morning after sunrise, the Master was walking down from the Rock of Prayer where we gathered to meditate in the early mornings. As usual, he took his time and stopped to talk to some brothers and sisters or to receive drawings from the children. This day he stopped in front of me, and without saying a word, his intense gaze penetrated me deeply. He seemed to see my whole life from A to Z. I heard within, "What have you been doing all this time? Come on, get to work." I said "Ok, Ok,

---

[24] Paneurhythmy is a danced composed and choreographed by Master Peter Deunov representing the steps of evolution in harmony with nature and the rhythm of the cosmos.

I'll get to work." It was all so crystal clear that I even wondered if I had answered out loud. Both question and answer seemed superimposed on me. For the next several days, I really tried to concentrate on the sunrise and practice the exercises recommended in one of his books, *The Splendour of Tiphareth*, which explains how to work on oneself while meditating at sunrise. I tried to stay focused and watched my thoughts closely. Every morning I tried to catch the sight of the Master to see if he was happy with my work. Not a sign. No food for the ego, for sure! It was perhaps a week or so later that he nodded in front of me on his descent from the Rock of Prayer, without even looking at me; just a very impersonal nod, as if to say: "Fine, keep going," but without any acknowledgment for the ego. Georg Feuerstein mentions this very experience in his book *The Mystery of Light*[25], with a few pertinent comments.

There was so much to learn, and amazingly, every lecture seemed to focus on the very subjects that were floating in my mind. One day the Master was talking about the fact that for Heaven we are like children and that children give their hand to their parents because they trust them. So that night I symbolically gave my hand to the Master in my mind's eye and asked him to protect me, to guide my soul and to take me all the way to God. In another lecture, he made reference to his own Master, Peter Deunov, and how he had so loved him and wanted to be like him that he ended up looking so much like him. That night I gave one hand to each Master, so I was sure not to get lost!! And then I went about asking questions of some close brothers and sisters about Master Peter Deunov. Was he still alive? Had he ever been to France? And I finally settled on the fact that if I had found the teaching of Omraam Mikhaël Aïvanhov first, it was because there was already a link between us. He was alive, from the West, modern, accessible, easy to understand, and I felt at home with all the elements of the Teaching. I also learned how he had come to look so much like Peter Deunov: by being

---

[25] *The Mystery of Light*, Georg Feuerstein, Passage Press, 1992, p. 80.

one with him. It is called the process of identification. So not only were they ONE in Spirit, but Mikhaël also bore witness to the power of his love for his Master.

On peoples' first visit to the Bonfin, they were invited to write a letter to the Master with a brief account of how they had discovered his Teachings, and to include a photo of themselves and put it in the mailbox by his garden. It took me about three weeks to make up my mind about it. Finally I wrote the letter, mentioning that while attending a yoga school we had read some of his books as part of the daily program, and that a picture of him in one of his books had stayed in my soul for several years until I found his Teachings and finally met my family of souls. Soon after, his secretary called out to me as we left the Great Hall following the Master's daily talk, saying that the Master wanted to meet with me in his garden the next day.

This is how I had the blessing to meet with the Master on that very first visit to the Bonfin. The day was so special; I dressed all in white for our meeting, and as I walked into his garden, I thought, *"I have found the Father of my Soul! Today is my wedding with Heaven."* Although I walked into the Master's garden with a sacred reverence, our meeting was very natural and simple. He was sitting at his garden table and asked a few questions about me, such as: "What is your profession? How old are you? Have you been reading my books?" Then he asked, "How can I be useful to you?" I said I would like to quit my work and live in the country with other brothers and sisters. After a moment of reflection during which he closed his eyes, he said in a very firm tone: "You must stay with the airline." I was rather perplexed and thought it must be my karma. I explained that the smoking on the planes bothered me (remember, this was 1981), and that First Class service, with the "French cut" meat bleeding and dripping from the cutting board, disturbed me to the point of causing me to nearly faint in the cabin (in those days, the service was quite elaborate and required cutting for each passenger). He said, "Don't worry, it will change soon." I then asked: "How can I serve the Teaching?" He asked what my possibilities were. I didn't quite know what to say, but an idea suddenly came to me: "I could bring some of your books to the West Coast of Canada, like Vancouver." He said: "Indeed, do that; and include the books on nutrition, sexuality and reincarnation. Everyone is concerned with these three subjects." He also asked, "Is anything else bothering you?" I mentioned to him that some months earlier I had been hit by a passenger on the airplane; I had to appear in court for the assault charges and feared for my safety. He became reflective for a moment and said: "Rest assured, it will take care of itself." He added a few more personal comments, and the meeting ended. Fifteen minutes had gone by, but it seemed we had covered so much. When I left his garden I felt so uplifted, as if I were walking on air. I was so light and happy! On the way to my room, I heard within myself: "Imagine everything you do being done by all human beings and ask yourself if that would bring about the Kingdom of God on Earth." A pretty powerful thought-seed and another way of measuring myself! Wanting to keep this feeling for as long as possible, I retreated to my room and didn't come out for several hours. I went over all the details of our meeting, engraving them in my soul.

Sure enough, over the next few months after meeting the Master, my issues with the airline were all resolved. I then made arrangements with the publisher Prosveta Canada to bring the books the Master had recommended to Vancouver where I had a layover: *The Yoga of Nutrition, Love & Sexuality* and *Man, Master of his Destiny*, the latter explaining how reincarnation made sense. I remember walking up to the French bookstore in downtown Vancouver called Le Bouquineur, so nervous and inexperienced at selling books. The store was painted blue and white, just like the colors of the buildings at the Bonfin. It stood next to a restaurant called *Côte D'Azur* (French Riviera). What a coincidence, I thought! I stopped at the bottom of the steps for a moment and connected with the Master, asking him to accompany me and put the words in my mouth. I suddenly felt so light going up the ten steps, as if I were levitating!

To my great surprise, the owner took all three books on consignment without hesitation. Within a few months, the whole collection was on their shelves. Another time, I took the same three titles to the main esoteric bookstore in Vancouver called Banyen Books. Again, to my surprise, the owner immediately accepted the Master's books, and since 1982 the store has carried them.

From then on, and for the next nine years, I worked for Prosveta as their representative in English Canada and served as a member on their Board of Directors. I used every layover possible in all Canadian cities the airline flew into and eventually opened some forty accounts with bookstores. Some of the esoteric bookstores even invited me to talk about the Teaching and introduce the books of the Master. So I gave a series of lectures over the years under the title "Initiatic Science."[26] I often showed a brief video of one of the Master's lectures and practiced the "laser meditation"[27] with the attendees.

Since 1981, I have gone to the Bonfin every year for a spiritual retreat. I call this my "rejuvenating time". After traveling year round for my work, it brings me great comfort to find myself in an ambiance of harmony, peace, joy and light. There I find the best food for all levels of existence: physical, mental, emotional and spiritual! The Bonfin is also a place where one works on purifying oneself, on purifying all our "bodies."

Purifying experience

Children are supported by their parents during youth, and there comes a time when self-sufficiency is required and

---

[26] It is the body of knowledge known to all great Masters, Sages and Initiates who recognize that the laws of the universe apply to nature and to human beings.

[27] The laser meditation is well explained in the pocket book entitled *Light is a Living Spirit* (Izvor Collection #209). It is a very powerful method requiring all participants to imagine and concentrate on a single object: the light.

parents give them space so they can grow and have their own experiences. And the same applies to the spiritual life: I had been inspired, supported and stimulated, and now a time of testing was knocking at my door. Usually I would arrive at the Bonfin tired, jet lagged, and in need of a few days for my subtle bodies to land and find their comfort before I felt grounded enough to open up to the energy of the place. On one particular visit, a strange feeling of negativity surrounded my thoughts, and I couldn't shake it off. Silly inner comments popped up about everything and everyone. I hated myself for it. One day, I was in the Great Hall with over five hundred brothers and sisters, and one of those negative thoughts came to mind about the Master while he was eating. Instantly, he raised his head and looked straight at me. I was seated somewhere in the middle of the Hall. I couldn't deny I was having those terrible thoughts, but how did he know these thoughts were from me? I said to myself, "I'm in trouble!" Why was I having such thoughts? Where did they originate from? I barely lasted the two weeks of my stay. I didn't sleep well, couldn't enjoy anything and was anxious to leave.

The day of my departure came. This was the only time ever, of all my visits, that I said to myself ... "finally!" On the way to the airport, my ticket to Amsterdam flew out the car window while I had my eyes closed. Back then there was no digital record, or cell phone. No ticket, no flight ... big trouble! After much negotiation, the only solution was to buy a full fare ticket. Needless to say, I also missed my connection from Amsterdam to Montreal and had to stay overnight in that city. In the past, a colleague had recommended a place, so I headed in that direction. Located above a noisy bar adjacent to the red light district, it was definitely the wrong place for me, and I was already so distressed. When I found bugs on the pillow, I asked for another room, and although I slept with the light on, I managed to have a nightmare during the little sleep I got. By the time I reached home, I was such a wreck. I cried my heart out. My nervous system was shattered, my face was like a field of strawberries ... so many pimples ... and my companion didn't know what to make of me. Later on, I was told by my Swiss friend Simone that sometimes we have to live through our 'garbage' in order to clear it out. This garbage, which might have accumulated in this lifetime or in a past one, sits in our soul memory, and as with a sink, when you pull the plug to change the water (changing your lifestyle), it stirs the debris from the bottom and brings it to the surface. Wow, did I have to do some cleansing! This period of negative thinking lasted several months. I found it difficult to meditate. I prayed hard and begged Heaven to give me some relief. I read everything I could find from the Teaching about negative states and entities and finally one day came across a passage in which the Master states that sometimes you cannot fight negativity yourself and must call on higher Beings to fight on your behalf. He had mentioned that brothers and sisters claimed to have been helped by him in the middle of the night through their ordeals, to which he answered: "Personally, I was sound asleep; it is the Beings who work with me, thousands of them who do the work." I decided I would talk to these higher Beings too and ask them to help me. One day, at last, my mind cleared and I was my happy self again. Thanks to Heaven ... literally! In hindsight, I understand that a Master has the right to test his students to see whether they will remain steadfast on the path or simply quit at the first obstacle. Walking the spiritual life is like choosing to climb a steep mountain in order to reach a high summit. Who would dare go without a guide? We know this on a physical level, but what about climbing the realms of the invisible world? Having the guidance of a Master does not change the difficulty of the terrain, but it will prevent many pitfalls and offer support and protection along the way.

Studying the Teaching

One after another, I took to reading the Master's books, underlining the passages that seemed important. By the time

I finished reading the two collections[28], two years had passed. As time went on, I re-read various books and came to realize that some passages I hadn't particularly noticed before would suddenly stand out. This gave me the honest feeling that my consciousness had shifted and expanded: it was another measuring stick. My understanding was deepening. With time, I also learned to recognize that the work of the soul and the spirit is like the seasons. Sometimes we live in the spring and wish it could last for eternity, but sometimes we find ourselves in a cold and dark winter. Isn't it an art to know how to use the different phases of our inner growth, and whether it is time to blossom or to retreat into our roots?

Simone, the same friend who had helped me understand the "cleansing" phase and whom I considered my "guardian angel", also invited me to reflect on the style of the Master's talks. For example, what kind of energy manifested through him when he spoke? What is the energy of love, of wisdom, or of power (power in the sense of stimulating us in our growth). Acquiring this discernment proved to be useful in my own life when dealing with different situations.

Simone was such a role model for me. She was on the Board of Directors of the Brotherhood in Switzerland, yet she was so humble, discreet, and always ready to help when needed. She was also funny with her magical sense of humor, her freckles and frizzy red hair. Sometimes, we would break up in laughter and other times find ourselves immersed in profound conversation. She brought such answers to my many questions. I even wondered sometimes what she found in me that motivated her to seek my company. She was older than me by two decades, yet it never seemed to faze her. She always remained accessible, knowledgeable without any arrogance or pride, and so steadfast in her love. Our friendship stood the test of time until she passed away in 1992. We met the first time I went to the Bonfin, and for

---

[28] The pocket book collection is called Izvor and the more detailed collection is called The Complete Works.

the next fourteen years we shared so much on so many levels, visiting each other in Canada, Switzerland or the Bonfin. After her passing, I asked Heaven what the link was that had created such a strong bond between us. In a meditation, I sensed that many, many lifetimes ago, she had asked to bear a child who had never known the light before and promised that if she became pregnant she would guide that being into the light. I sensed that she had been my mother then, and I cried with love and compassion at this revelation. It felt so deeply engrained in my being. Still to this day, when I relive this memory, tears well up in me. She has been a ray of light in my life.

But let us come back to the study of this wonderful Teaching. The more I read the books, the more answers I received, yet it is so vast and reaches so many levels that one can never fully know it completely. For example, in the book entitled *Cosmic Moral Laws*[29] I found answers to questions about injustices in the world, about why we exist and where we go from here. I discovered the law of affinity and how creative the thought process is.

One of the most vital lessons for students on a spiritual path is recognizing that all of us are endowed with a dual nature: the "personality" and the "individuality". The personality is linked to the ego, the egocentric nature which is always looking out for its own interest; and the individuality, the higher Self, is the selfless nature, always loving, compassionate and the seat of our intuition. To practice the daily exercise of examining our thoughts, feelings and actions in the light of this criterion is vitally important for one's growth, and for avoiding unnecessary obstacles along the way.

Now being under the guidance of a spiritual Master gave me a protection, a constant awareness, a direction and essential purpose in my life: to work on the purity of my thoughts, feelings and actions, and to manifest a behavior that reflected these values. When I live in harmony with my higher Self, I open

---

[29] Omraam Mikhaël Aïvanhov, Complete Works, Vol. #12, Prosveta S.A.

myself to greater realms of spiritual connection with others and the world.

The Master visits North America in the 1980s

During the eighties, the Master came to North America several times: to Los Angeles, New York and Quebec. When visiting Quebec, he would stay for one month or so, giving lectures on the weekends to large groups of people at various Brotherhood centers throughout the province. I was always sad when I had to fly while he was visiting. One of these times, when he was staying at the Radost Center near where I lived, I had a flight to Edmonton, Alberta. We were on final descent to the airport while a thunderstorm was developing on the horizon. Suddenly we hit wind shear (wind currents that precede a storm) with a force. The aircraft was nearly out of control. Although I was strapped in my jump seat with shoulder harnesses and seat belt, my legs and arms flew upward. I was pressed hard between the wall and the jump seat as we dropped 1000 feet very quickly. The aircraft banked completely to the left, then abruptly to the right. I could see the ground below! There was another sudden drop, and my head and neck pressed into my shoulders. People were screaming in the cabin. Then an overwhelming force came over me, and I called out the name of the Master, OMRAAM MIKHAËL AÏVANHOV, three times. The aircraft came back barely under control with the pilots constantly correcting the banking for a safe landing. Then we dropped again and eventually roughly hit the runway. People were paralyzed in their seats. Finally, once everyone had disembarked, the Captain immerged from the cockpit, his shirt totally soaked to the waist, and said: "Consider yourselves lucky we made it." In all my years of flying, it was the closest I had ever come to a crash. The other crewmembers didn't say a word at first, but eventually admitted they thought it was the end for them. Leaving the airport for our hotel, we all fell silent. Surely we were all counting our blessings. The next morning, the Captain said that wind shear, undetectable by radar in those days, was often the cause of crashes on takeoff or landing. I held in my heart the feeling that it was calling on the Master that allowed us to survive that situation.

In 1984, on another of the Master's visit to Canada, I was in the air when his flight from Paris was approaching. I wanted so much to meet him at the Mirabel International Airport. There would be other brothers and sisters there as well, but my flight was arriving at the domestic airport in Dorval. I asked inwardly to receive a sign when the Master's flight touched down so I could be there in thought with those welcoming him. On my drive home, I noticed a full rainbow overarching the sun. I thought to myself, what is this phenomenon? Could it be that the Master has just arrived! This is beyond imagination! I felt such a sudden surge of joy. It was incredible. It was confirmed later that indeed the Master had arrived at that precise moment.

Around the same time I was offered a permanent position working on the Prosveta staff. There was a lot going on in my life, including efforts to sell my house in St Placide and the closing of the airline's Montreal base, which would require me to relocate, commute or quit. I thus was hesitant to accept the offer, but at the same time I longed to be of deeper service to the Brotherhood. Fortunately for me, the Master was still in Canada for a few more weeks, staying near where I lived, and the president of Prosveta Canada arranged for me to have another meeting with him.

Once with the Master, I summarized our first meeting and thanked him for his wonderful guidance. I then told him about the offer from Prosveta and my desire to serve the Teaching, and that the airline was going through some major changes which would require me to commute to Toronto or move to another base. The Master listened intently and said, "When we first met, you were new and I told you what was best for you then, but by now you should have the criteria of the Teaching. Have you been reading my books? If so, you should be able to decide what is best. For example, consider the position you are being offered and ask yourself whether you would have the best conditions for your blossoming. Then consider the conditions you have now and ask yourself whether you already have the best ones for your blossoming." He also asked who would support me financially if I were to work for Prosveta. I said my companion John would do so (by then we had been together seven years, and he had agreed to support me should I leave the airline). After reflecting a brief moment, the Master said it was better to earn some money for oneself. During that meeting, the Master spoke to me on different subjects that appeared to be disparate. For example, he said: "Learn to express yourself properly, you will need it" and then jumped to the subject of the arid conditions of the desert, expounding on the date tree that produces the sweetest fruits. I didn't quite know why he spoke so elaborately about this. But nearly a decade later I understood why, when my life had become like a desert. His "spirit" had foreseen the soul journey I would have to undergo.

After that meeting with the Master, which was also my last one, I retreated again to my room and went over his every word. I kept hearing his statement, "Choose what is best for your blossoming."

Still filled with the Master's presence, I had to establish enough peace within myself to sense where these best conditions were. I wanted to see things the way he did. After deep reflection, I began to see that I had quite a bit of freedom with the airline, not only in terms of time off, but also during layovers. Once in a hotel room, I could rest, meditate and read to my liking. I could still represent Prosveta when appropriate, make new friends and also stay in touch with brothers and sisters throughout the world. As a permanent staff member at Prosveta, I would be bound by office work nine-to-five, five days a week. Despite my need to be of service, this made me feel tight inwardly to the point of discomfort. I also remembered that I had not enjoyed the nine-to-five routine after the yoga school. The Master was right: I already had the best conditions for my blossoming. How could I serve the Teaching if I weren't happy?

A true Master knows the essential truths according to Cosmic Intelligence. He also has the ability and the will to control everything within himself, and he uses this knowledge and control solely to manifest the qualities and virtues of disinterested love. He doesn't use others for the benefit of himself or the organization. On the contrary, his scope is far beyond the immediate rewards. His only interest is the evolution of a person's soul and the divine manifestation of the spirit.

Once it was clear in my mind that I had to go on with my flying career, my house in St. Placide sold very quickly to a young man by the name of Serge. He had suffered a severe car accident several months before and had been hospitalized with broken legs and pelvis. He said he had seen a being of Light at the scene of the accident and didn't know what to make of it. When he came to visit my house as a potential buyer, he saw the photo of the Master above the fireplace and asked who it was. I said he was my spiritual Master, a being of Light who was guiding me in my inner development. He was stunned! He said he had been saved in the accident by a being of Light who looked just like him. We had a long talk about spiritual matters. He came back to see the house again and purchased it. We saw each other on several occasions after that. It was so reassuring to realize that the house had not sold until then because I first needed to see the Master again and to clarify my own situation. Also, Heaven had its own reasons, and choosing to serve involves so many different factors.

So from 1984 to 1990 I commuted to Toronto as my new base and continued to represent Prosveta. I flew both domestic and international flights. One day on a flight to Buenos Aires, my colleague and friend, Francine, asked if I were ever scared while flying. I knew she was reading the books of the Master, so I didn't mind sharing on a deeper level. I told her the story of the near crash in Edmonton when I had called out the Master's name three times, and that somehow I had not been afraid since. We were in the crew bus on our way to the hotel after a twelve hour flight when I explained: "Look Francine, I haven't shared this story with many people, and I don't have proof, just a strong conviction that it was because I called out the name of the Master that we didn't crash. I profoundly sense that as long as I keep my link with the Master, I will be protected. If I am wrong, I will be reprimanded by Heaven, but if I am right, I will receive a sign."

Buenos Aires is known as a rather smoggy city. You can rarely see the sun, even at its zenith. We arrived at the hotel around noon and were truly jet-lagged. As we waited for our crew bags to be offloaded, I happened to look up in the sky, and what did I see? A full rainbow around the sun! It was only slightly hazy that day, so the rainbow was clearly visible. I tugged at Francine's uniform sleeve and said, "See, I told you I would get a sign if it were true! Look at this rainbow around the sun. How often have you seen that? It is one of the signs I receive that confirms the Master's presence. What I told you is true. This is the sign!" I was so charged with energy, I broke into a sweat and felt as if I were plugged into a 550 volt current! Despite my extreme fatigue, I was overflowing with joy and an incredible surge of energy, and I couldn't fall sleep for quite some time. The aura of a Master is so large, so vast, that it encompasses those connected with him wherever they are. I now knew this beyond any doubt.

Departure of the Master: Christmas 1986

In December of 1986, the departure of the Master for the other world came as a shock to many of us, although some brothers and sisters said later on that they had had dreams or signs. My companion John and I were visiting friends of the Brotherhood in Vancouver when we heard the news of his passing. It was Christmas time, and the moon was full. How would we fare without his presence? What would happen to the Brotherhood? Would someone want to replace him? Had we become so used to him physically that we wouldn't be able to function as well without him? None of us knew ... we had to wait and see.

It is interesting that the Master Peter Deunov also left at a similar time of the year, on December 27, 1944, in a very conscious manner and just before the communists came to interrogate him.

Another curious fact is that Vancouver had recorded the highest wave activity of any full moon in history on that day. A friend who is a keen astrologer mentioned that there was a very favorable conjuncture of planets at that precise date. I believe the Master left in full consciousness at a well-chosen time to continue his work from the other side. In hindsight, some of his last lectures hinted at his departure.

I remember hearing a lecture at the Bonfin in which the Master mentioned that some of the great Saints and Masters had died of various illnesses. He mentioned St. Francis of Assisi, Shivananda and Ramakrishna, among others. He said they were not paying their own karma with such illnesses, but taking on the liberation of others through the sacrifice of their body. Yogananda mentions in his *Autobiography of a Yogi*[30]: "On rare occasions ... a Master who wishes to quicken greatly his disciples' evolution may then voluntarily work out on his own body a large measure of their undesirable karma."

Yogananda also mentions that when Jesus shed his blood for the redemption of the world, what he had actually done was to cleanse humanity's astral body from impurities with the purity of his own blood, thereby clearing the path between the astral realm and a higher consciousness.

I also believe the Master sacrificed his body to free humanity from its cancerous state. So many clairvoyants, seers and prophets have predicted terrible events destined to cleanse

[30] Paramahansa Yogananda, published by Self-Realization Fellowship, Los Angeles, USA. 1979 edition, p. 236.

humanity and the planet. If we have been spared so far, I believe it is the result of the sacrifices of such great Masters. Their ultimate choices not only open the path to the invisible realm but create extra time for humanity's awakening to accelerate, which helps restore balance to the planet's energy and helps Mother Earth to regenerate.

As it turns out, after the Master's departure most of the brothers and sisters were mature enough to keep working on their development without seeking to replace the being who had guided them on their journey towards perfection. The presidents of the Brotherhood centers around the world have held to the direction given by the Master, guarding the spirit of the Teaching. These centers are luminous focal points where one nourishes the soul and fortifies the spirit while radiating light onto the world through the songs, laser meditation and other methods. No one has tried to replace the Master, for such a cosmic being is not born every day ... not even every century.

Personally, I carried on with my activities as before, relying even more on my intuition and inner guidance. I moved to Vancouver in 1992 following more changes in the airline (the only constant in the airline is change ...). And as predicted by the Master nearly a decade earlier, I went into an arid desert that lasted seven years, after which life smiled on me. I met the love of my life, Jim, who eventually became my husband. He is a wonderful companion, and we share many things in common. Jim has embraced the Teaching with all his heart and supports me in my spiritual development and activities, as I do him.

In 2011, I was gifted with a vision of the Master on the Rock of Prayer in the Bonfin that inspired me to coordinate and jointly author the Aquarian Team's first book, *What the Future of Humanity Could Be!* A few months later, I was interviewed about it on YouTube by the host Lilou Mace of Juicy Living Tours, who interviews people about their experiences of personal growth.

Today, thanks to social media and to dedicated brothers and sisters, several websites present the biography and works of

Master Omraam Mikhaël Aïvanhov in an easily accessible format. One can even listen to extracts of his lectures on YouTube. This enables those who feel inundated with news about corruption, terrorism, greed and pollution to find a breath of fresh air and new hope for their future.

The last message of the Master

Before the Master left, he prepared a message for the Brotherhood: "Know that I am with you always," which meant that although his work was completed on Earth and he was now able to do even greater work in the invisible world, he was not abandoning us. By connecting with our own higher Self, we can be in touch with a teacher's super-consciousness and feel this being even more so than if he were in a physical body.

To have the opportunity to meet a living Master is indeed a tremendous blessing. What is most important is to find inspiration, stimulation and a deeper bond with Heaven through a Master's teachings. And one's sense of appreciation, love and respect for such a teaching provide as great an opportunity to grow to another level of consciousness as being physically close to a Master, if not even more so.

On the path of self-development, nothing stops us from imitating those who have surpassed us. It is said in Initiatic Science that love is a fusion, and through fusion, or identification, we commune with the being we love. This is how the Master understood and interpreted Jesus' words: he identified with him in order to fully understand his Teaching.[31]

In an authentic Initiatic School, the disciple is invited to discover the different levels of inner work: reflection, which is the process of thinking; meditation, a work of the mind which explores a subject; contemplation, an activity of the heart which focuses one's feelings on something, such as the beauty of a rose,

[31] See *The true meaning of Christ's Teaching*, Izvor collection #215 Prosveta. ISBN:978-2-85566-322-7

or a sunrise; and lastly, identification, the process of fusing with the subject or being we want to become one with. The Master had demonstrated this faculty by identifying with Master Peter Deunov, to the point of looking remarkably like him. The key to identification is love: the shortest path to God.

Master Omraam said he was merely a signpost for us, that it was up to us to follow its direction and do the walking, that the Teaching covers every aspect of life, that we must rely only on our inner work, that we are to apply the criteria of the Teaching in order to find our answers and foster a high ideal that will guide and transform our life. He summarized all the key themes in the last season of his lectures: health and nutrition, purity and sexuality, politics and synarchy, spirit and matter. For fifty years he had described a large selection of methods for people to choose from in order to improve their lives, to grow and perfect themselves.

All those who work to align themselves with their higher Self and to spread the light on Earth have their names written in the Book of Life, whatever movement or organization they belong to. When people in great enough numbers awaken to the fact that they are first and foremost souls and spirits and consciously decide to focus their energy on a high ideal, on the goal of bringing about a Golden Age, we will experience a garden of paradise on Earth.

Carmen Froment's biography:

Thanks to the airline and the advice of my spiritual guide and Master, I travel around the world, teach paneurhythmy, visit different brotherhood centers and meet fantastic people. There is a perfect opportunity on my flights to serve on a higher level by linking the crew and the passengers to the light and to Heaven, inviting their consciousness to expand for the realization of a Golden Age on Earth.

Through the years I have witnessed incredible changes taking place, leading us toward a more global, more universal and soon more fraternal world. I am infinitely grateful to this Being who oriented me towards my best direction in this lifetime, and for the methods he taught which allow me to blossom on all levels: Omraam Mikhaël Aïvanhov.

Carmen wrote on Politics, Evolution and Involution, and the Golden Age in the first book and was also the coordinator.

CHAPTER 5

Bertrand's journey

"The Breath of Spirit," "Sublime Love" ... there are words, phrases lying dormant deep within us, well hidden beyond our awareness. Yet unbeknownst to us, these words stir us, inspire us through the years, until one day we hear or read them, and, resonating in the depths of our being, they mark the start of a great adventure in the realm of the soul. They were waiting to be revealed, and it is often in encounters with others, who act as mirrors for us, that what has been hidden from our full awareness becomes alive to us. At that moment, we realize the aspirations of our soul, of our inner being.

Quite often, it is only years later that we become aware of these images asleep deep within. Sleeping is not the right word, as they are more like smoldering embers awaiting the right moment to ignite. It may happen at once, like lightning, a sudden revelation, a grace from above, or through meeting someone, or by way of a conference, a movie, a melody, a book or a dream—any means by which Heaven sees fit to wake us up—but it can also happen in a progressive way. One after another, the veils lift, revealing a secret and precious part of our inner being. That is how it happened for me. No instant lightning, no fire suddenly bursting forth.

We were fortunate, my brothers and I, to live in a family where both love and discipline reigned. Our parents chose to live in a villa in a Paris suburb. It was a modest villa but it had a garden, which allowed us to have a dog throughout our childhood. This link with an animal quickly helped me understand that not only did I love animals, but also that so many adults do not really consider them as living beings worthy of our love and attention. I noticed that some people mistreated them; they beat them as if they were things and not living beings with a right to live life well. Many adults behaved as if animals were there merely for their own pleasure, their personal satisfaction.

In my youth, this attitude I saw in adults saddened me, and I took refuge in the closeness I shared with our dog. Sometimes revolt would brew inside me, because I could not understand this egoistic attitude, this disdain and disregard for animals. One day, during a walk in a forest with my parents, this acknowledgement of the life in our brothers, the animals, led me to ask my mother a question: "Why do we kill animals and then eat them?" I was about five or six at the time and found it easiest to confide in my mother. That question came straight from my heart, as my mind could not understand such acts. I was not very talkative, but I had long reflected on this issue without finding an answer. Finally I resorted to uttering my question with the naiveté of a child. My mother kindly explained that eating meat was necessary to the good development and health of children during their growing years, and it was also beneficial to human beings in general. It was natural, almost mandatory. Oh yes, in those years, it was almost an undisputed fact. The truths of an epoch are often only relative ones. In short, it was around the age of twenty that I became aware that vegetarianism did indeed exist and that vegetarians are very healthy as long as they keep to a well-balanced diet. So, I decided overnight not to eat animals ... and my conscience felt a lot better for it!

However, it was not that easy! This is when I verified the law of inertia, or, in psychological terms, the law of entrainment; not all my cells were in agreement with that decision—some had definitely become used to a meat diet. Even if I had said yes in my mind and in my heart, a part of my nature that had been fed animal products was rebelling. During the first year, I dreamed occasionally that I was still eating meat! Then it was over; my cells were free of these astral images, of these old patterns, as if the *tail* had finally followed through where the head had gone. Just as the tail of a snake always ends up entering the same hole the head went in, so with a bit of perseverance and willpower, everything ends up following through when a decision is made.

I learned later on that this law is found everywhere in life and most interestingly in our inner life. Even when we know that something is preferable, when we wish for it with all our heart and even want it with all our might, it is only by keeping a steadfast pace in that direction that, little by little, our entire being commits to it. This requires a lot of time. If we analyze ourselves, we realize that we are far from living life to the fullest. It is extremely rare that our whole being participates in any action whatsoever. I only saw this in those who are justifiably called *Masters*: they are masters of themselves, and all of their being is an ongoing symphony. But I am ahead of myself! The fact is that at our level we easily notice that we want to improve, but there is a certain inertia before the entire machine takes the new direction. Knowing this law helps us to better understand and manage our life in terms of what we truly desire.

So I was nurturing this love for nature and especially for the animals, but I also needed to understand … to understand the laws that govern us and the world in which we are immersed, our universe. This is why at school I became interested in all scientific disciplines: math, physics and chemistry. For me, they represented something more reliable, more truthful and more real than the other disciplines. Something *tangible*, logical, where one could follow reasoning, explain a phenomenon and demonstrate such and such a mathematical *truth*. I liked going to the heart of things … at least I thought so, but this is where it gets complicated. At first, I did not realize it, as I was busy discovering, doing experiments, learning to manage equations to deepen my quest: exploring the roots of it all. Being accepted into *Mat Sup* and then into *Math Spé* (a higher school preparatory class) was a sheer delight! To be sure, it was challenging to spend part of my youth locked up in my room or in class every day including weekends—no more sports at the gym I had attended from the time I was young—but I was happy to see that everything I had studied until then was being demonstrated. Yet, despite this joy, this satisfaction, I kept feeling inwardly that the Truth was missing; there was still a void to be filled.

One night at around the age of fifteen or sixteen, when I had entered high school and seriously begun to apply myself academically, I was about to fall asleep when a 'presence' who had kept me company since childhood left me. It made me understand that it could no longer stay with me because of the studies I was about to begin—engineering in a *Grande École* which is a prestigious higher education establishment outside the main framework of the French university system. I was very sad to feel this presence leave me, even though deep down I knew it had to be that way. Invisible friends accompany all of us, and they need distinctive conditions in order to stay with us— such as purity, love, harmony—each presence having a specific affinity. To engage in a certain domain may draw our friends away for a time, and it can also attract others. Later on, when a cycle is completed, after having acquired certain elements, we can regain that state in which our past friends can come back, perhaps accompanied by others, and it is then even more beautiful, as we feel richer than before. It is a matter of making a sacrifice for a certain period in order to acquire experiences and capabilities—or it may be part of paying off some karma!

In my youth I felt different from many of my peers, as if I were out of step with them. I did not share the same tastes, nor did I enjoy the same pleasures as they did. And even if I had friends whom I saw often, I regularly needed to withdraw and spend time by myself. I could not confide in anyone and always had the impression I was out of sync with their activities, except in sports.

Today, many young people may share this same feeling. It is in fact the soul that, knowing other worlds and vaguely remembering them, keeps seeking a greater awareness of itself, without fully understanding what is going on. The soul expects such *different* conditions! It knows that life is quite different from what we are led to believe and see everywhere in the movies, the commercials, the news. It does not recognize itself in such an artificial and superficial world, and so, without the connection with the soul, one feels deprived of something still unknown, prey to a malaise of sorts, an unidentifiable void. I am convinced that waves of souls incarnate in some epochs with a program, and that presently many of the young are here to help bring peace, harmony, beauty and respect for all life to the planet, even if they are not yet conscious of their role. They are not aware of what they agreed to do before incarnating. Meeting someone or reading a book can lift the veil, and then life takes on an extraordinary meaning, becomes full of light, and the person is ready to walk the path—the path where his or her soul shines.

Although I had invested myself in scientific studies, I was still open to many things. Just as much as I wanted to understand tangible realities, I needed to lift the veil over phenomena disregarded by science. A few special friends and I had been interested in hypnosis for awhile and held some sessions together, which I don't recommend at all because of potential danger. In any case, one of those experiences made me reflect profoundly on the notions of freedom, consciousness and reality. That day, one of us had been h*ypnotized*, and after some classical experiments, we had the idea to program him before waking him up. We were in a school building at the end of a hallway leading to many classrooms. All the classrooms were empty, and we were the only people there. This is what we suggested to our hypnotized friend: "We will wake you up. We will leave the building together, and as we go by the last classroom, you will be unable to stop yourself from leaving us and entering that last classroom. If we ask you about your motivation, you will answer very naturally that you needed to check to see if you were in there. And you will be convinced that you are acting in complete freedom, fully aware of yourself and conscious of your thoughts." The whole thing was so absurd that we hardly believed it would work. But guess what happened? Everything unfolded according to the programming! When we told him afterwards, "Come on, don't you realize how absurd this is, both what you did and your answer? This can't be really you." "Yes, yes, I assure you, I truly felt like checking to see if I was in that classroom."

This raises the question, where does true reality lie? Who can be sure that, right now, I am not asleep or being manipulated? These kinds of questions were really a concern for me; I could sense some parts of the answers, but only later on would I feel the immensity of what they entailed. Only by studying the science of life, in a true esoteric teaching of life (esoteric in the sense of inner, as in the inner side of life, in contrast to the purely objective, external side, accessible to the five senses), does one discover what is concealed within this kind of questioning. And how does one study this new science without a teacher, a guide? Books can be useful, but a mountain guide remains indispensable when tackling new summits.

In the first year of college, we had a teacher of physics and chemistry who was remarkable and amazing. From the very onset, he established order in the classroom with a genuine and kind authority. He would never raise his voice. Even the disturbing students (there are always some in any class) sensed something special about him. Very quickly we all acknowledged his qualities as a teacher and as a pedagogue. His classes were clear, rich, illustrated and captivating, but above all, he would introduce here and there small elements that would broaden the field of application of the laws he was explaining. A law in physics that elucidated such and such phenomena would also be found in other areas of life (biology, psychology, feelings, intellect, etc). Thus, with him I began to perceive a greater synthesis of life.

81

Since he remained very discrete and offered only small hints, two of my classmates and I wanted to meet with him at the end of the class to chat and ask him questions. We were drawn to him without really knowing why. At first we would ask him questions about physics and his lessons, and then little by little about increasingly broader subjects. Even when he was no longer our teacher, we continued to visit him from time to time throughout our senior year and beyond. He eventually suggested that we visit him at his place. There were only two of us then. Slowly, he opened our heart and consciousness to vaster horizons, more and more spiritual, but what was wonderful is that he never launched into dreamy discourses; on the contrary, he always remained based in the laws of nature, in logic, observation and common sense. Something beyond his words always resonated deeply in us. That, in fact, was his most important quality. When you meet someone who inspires trust and with whom you feel comfortable, who explains things in a crystal clear way, who awakens in you a greater sense of humanity, a greater desire to love and help others and to respect life in all its multiple forms, and when you go home feeling enthusiastic, inspired and more alive, that man or woman is showing you the right path. Do not hesitate. Listen and learn from such a person who has acquired a segment of the truth and behaves according to cosmic laws. This is what we felt at the time, without being able to put words to it.

One day in particular, when my friend and I were visiting him, I asked: "You say that when one wants to study a particular field in depth, it is preferable, prior to launching oneself alone into new discoveries, to learn the current state of knowledge from a professor. If we were to start from scratch, it is not even certain that in a single lifetime we would rediscover, for example, that the water molecule is constituted of two atoms of hydrogen and one atom of oxygen. Only after that could we expect to carry on the research towards new discoveries. Professor, you have a lot of knowledge about Life, do you not have someone who instructs you?" The idea that someone was inspiring my professor felt so natural. Otherwise, how could he demonstrate so much wisdom and humanity, seemingly based on a profound knowledge? This question triggered the opening of new doors.

As I write these lines, the story of Parsifal in the legend of the Holy Grail comes to mind. Steiner explains that Parsifal, seeing for the first time the holy cup in the castle, should have dared to ask questions. It would have spared him many years and much suffering in his quest. Eventually, the moment came when he was ready. Expressing the right kind of questions acts like a trigger; it is a quest that begins in the mental plane, then move to the emotional plane until it reaches down to the physical one where it is ready to be manifested. It was from that moment on that my professor felt *allowed* to speak to us about the teaching of Master Omraam Mikhaël Aïvanhov. He had been following his Teaching for years. He played a cassette of one of his lectures, and while my friend listened with attention, my whole being shivered at the sound of his voice, his intonations, his words. Far more than the exactness and beauty of the talk, it was the life that flowed through the Master's words that touched me. Something secret and sacred resonated with this source flowing into my soul, and it felt like an awakening, a wake-up call. I kept everything deep within myself, though, not yet realizing the full impact of everything that, unbeknownst to me, began stirring inside. But I believe that my professor, knowledgeable about human nature and attentive to subtle signs, had sensed what had been triggered.

I began purchasing and reading some of the books of this Master and was moved by truths that opened a new world in which everything makes sense and where nothing is left to chance. The explanations I had been looking for were revealed, and I understood that the world obeys laws one must know in order to move forward. An immense light seemed to radiate from these books, an immense and disinterested love directed towards all humanity and even all of creation. Later on I understood that what characterizes great beings is this very disinterestedness, this unconditional love that endlessly flows like a spring, guided by wisdom and the knowledge of universal, cosmic laws.

I noticed how everything was alive for this Master, even the rocks, the trees, the stars. However, I kept this part of my life secret, because on one hand I had to dedicate myself fully to completing my studies, which claimed a lot of time and energy, and on the other hand, because I could not envision joining this spiritual school: I did not feel worthy of it. Given the Teaching, and the fact this Master was a being of such an elevated consciousness, I imagined that his disciples could only be beings of light, nearly angelical. So in view of my shortcomings, it seemed pointless even to think of it.

My studies went well. I was successful in the entrance exams for a few reputable engineering schools and entered one of them. In the final year, I found that another set of circumstances was waiting for me. Who can deny that our life obeys laws often beyond our own awareness? For me a time of silent and subconscious maturation was necessary. A certain work occurs in the dark before a seed emerges to pursue its growth out in the open, exposed to the warm rays of the sun.

I had a group of friends, and one of them was a girl to whom I felt very attracted because of what she emanated, and because of her natural, simple way of being. A light seemed to emanate from her, and she was so different from everyone else. Then I learned she was a member of a spiritual teaching and practiced meditation. I began pondering all of this, remembering my high school teacher. One evening I had an impulse to call this girl and said to her, "I would like to become a member of the spiritual movement you follow."

Thus began a new life! I prayed ardently to be accepted, and this time my soul had priority over my timidity. I was moving ahead!

The first meeting with a true Master will always be one of the most precious moments in a disciple's life. The first time I attended one of his lectures was on a Sunday at Izgrev, one of the brotherhood centers near Paris. After the lecture, I was invited to meet him in the small hall, and in situations such as this, so many things happen in the invisible world. For me the first meeting was beyond words, time and space. It took place far beyond the realm of ordinary consciousness and the physical plane; it was sacred and magical. In India they say that it is not the disciple who chooses his Master, but the Master who calls on his disciple when the time has come.

Why is a Master so desirable in the life of a person who wants to grow and progress? I have already touched on this subject, but now I could add that, in fact, everyone has already one or even many masters. Hubert Mansion's film[32] summarizes it very well. For some, their master will be the need for power, while for others it is the need for riches, glory or social recognition. All of us are drawn to act according to an entity, an egregore, an idea or a physical person. Because this is so, we might as well make use of a true light to guide our life toward a sublime Idea, a lofty Ideal that can manifest itself in the form of a being incarnated in the physical plane, serving as a model for us. In the Western world, this notion of a Master is little recognized or accepted, whereas in the Eastern world, many people yearn to find a true Master.

Why can a Master serve as a model? The simple reason is that he is master of himself. Thanks to his knowledge of the laws that govern the universe, thanks to the love he is capable of manifesting towards all creatures (humans, including his worst enemies, but also animals, vegetables, minerals, without forgetting the countless spiritual entities of the celestial hierarchies), he has attained mastery over his whole being: his physical body, his feelings and his thoughts. This true mastery is such a rare accomplishment. It is a blessing when we encounter

---

[32] *In A Master's Presence, a* film directed by Hubert Mansion and Emy Tamko, 2013, Gamahae, available as DVD.

such a being, inspiring us to take him as a model, to listen to him and follow his philosophy of life.

To say that afterwards life becomes 'all roses' is not quite accurate; difficulties, trials and obstacles continue to exist, and sometimes we feel as if they are even magnified! But, like a student sitting on a school bench, we take this opportunity to practice the lessons learned and take our exams. What is new is the understanding. We feel better equipped and have a variety of methods at our disposal to face new situations. We have the impression we are living in an accelerated mode, learning in one year what would otherwise have taken a lifetime!

Nevertheless, for me the first year unfolded amazingly. The discovery of a new way of thinking, of behaving and of loving all made me live beyond time. Blessings kept pouring over me, and my consciousness travelled in regions yet unknown to me. I later understood that this was a kind of light shed on what awaits us all on the path. I felt like a newborn on earth, seeing only beauty everywhere. And I attracted it! I believe this is what protected me in the beginning, because I lacked the knowledge and skills to see human nature in its different aspects. One must be strong to see things as they are; that is why clairvoyance can be such a burden!

How can one describe those intense moments spent during the summer congresses, continuously bathing in the Master's aura? Words cannot describe the ambiance that uplifted us day and night. I felt as if I were on board a large white sailboat whose captain navigated us to new horizons, ever more beautiful. It was as if I were bathing in a river of life, the water penetrating deep inside my every cell, every atom, bearing life, enthusiasm, and pure white Christic light. And this happened as much during the demanding work (maintenance of buildings, construction projects, agriculture and preparation of meals ...) as during the meditations, the singing, the moments of silence in the great hall, the meals taken in silence, and the talks the Master gave several times a day. Everything unfolded in perfect harmony in his presence; it was life manifesting itself, bountiful, wholesome. He talked to us about the new life to come for all of humanity, and we had the good fortune to preview and savor it, to feel it and bear witness to it!

All this remains for me a fantastic benchmark of what life can be. The Master would say: "Here we enjoy the first fruits of the Golden Age, this age that is coming to Earth, in which there will be no more wars, no more misery, and no more famine." I want to believe in that future in which humanity will recognize itself as one great family and will develop in the subtle realms of existence. Yet, through the years I have realized that nice words alone will not change things; for example, doesn't everyone have a sincere wish for peace? However, this obviously does not suffice as long as our consciousness remains asleep. This is why I am so weary of all the *New Age* fads that make everything seem so easy to attain, almost without efforts; I do not share this belief. The awakening of consciousness is a long winding path, with many successive phases, requiring many efforts. The Master used to tell us that only a few people would join his school because it requires such great work on oneself in order to profoundly change something within.

In the presence of the Master, even apart from him, we each received tremendous blessings. Every day he greeted us and bombarded us with powerful rays of pure love, especially after the meditation we practiced together every morning at dawn on a rock facing the rising sun. Such beauty in this simple greeting, yet such a powerful, gesture! Thus I understood how every day we could exchange this light, energy and love among ourselves, simply with our hand, without even touching each other. I know that one day it will be common practice, when we will be aware of the incredible possibilities hidden behind the slightest daily gesture. According to the Master, a conscious being or a true spiritual Master who raises the hand towards the sun gains, in a just few moments, the equivalent of an entire lifetime of spiritual gifts. How many riches do we bypass without even being aware of them! We are unconscious of the treasures right beside our path, like someone who sleeps in a room filled with gold coins but who is unable to see this wealth within reach.

We are able to go on receiving all of these treasures through the Master's agency and the gift of his presence, and even those who have never met him on the physical plane can also experience this. What is required of us is that we have a sincere desire to evolve, to grow, and to nurture that desire with love. Just as the most beautiful things have their origin in the subtle, invisible world, so we can open ourselves each day to the sun and to the presence of a true Master. There are many Masters/teachers who have not abandoned our earth but who live in the sun, linked to that great unknown, that mysterious Land of the Living mentioned in the Bible.

In fact, the Master instructed us even more so in the invisible realms, particularly during the night, even when he was with us during the summer congresses. In the same way, disciples can continue to be instructed at night when we travel in our subtle bodies and join this being who is our model and reference. Can't two people in love visit each other even when separated by thousands of kilometers? Love is beyond space and lifts us to other realms. Before we fall asleep, it is up to each of us to set our intention to join the beings we love or to choose to attend the 'divine school'. Many young people who entered this school of life after the Master's departure have had the opportunity to experience privileged moments where they have met him and received essential keys from him. The memory of it sometimes remains intact or at other times only leaves an impression upon waking, as the intellect can distort the images as the soul re-enters the physical body.

Love. Here we are again, at the heart of a fundamental question! For each of us, male or female, love is a subject that marks our life. The Master spoke about love in a way I had never heard or read before. He introduced us to dimensions of it unknown to us, helping us to approach the immensity of the subject, far beyond our religious, moral or societal conceptions. He spoke to us about divine, sublime love, not only between two beings, but also towards all creatures and all of creation. Love is at the basis of the entire universe; it is the very essence of creation, the *glue* that guarantees the universe's cohesion, from the atoms to the galaxies. "Let the water flow, just love," he liked to tell us, and then everything else will come at the right time, at the right place. Yes, but what kind of love?

Once we understand that loving in the lower regions of our being feeds entities of the lower astral plane, larvae, (monsters that we do not see, of course, but who feed on our energies), we feel the need to improve our approach to life and want to live differently.

When I was studying in Canada, I regularly shopped at an organic food store where I admired a young girl who worked there. I liked going there often, sometimes buying almost nothing and not even talking to the girl, only seeking contentment in her subtle emanations. Perhaps it also had to do with my shyness! One day I was mesmerized and overjoyed: I *saw* a most beautiful light, an extraordinary emanation flowing from her chest, despite the very decent neckline of her blouse. That feminine fluid filled me with immense joy, and I could better understand why we men are attracted to women. What we are searching for is mainly an essence, an emanation, a fluid, a life beyond appearances, and that experience was very important to me.

I had the chance to experience this while young, thanks to knowledge of the Teaching, and I wish for all young people to experience this at least once. And Heaven had something else in store for me. A few days later (or perhaps the next day, I don't remember anymore), during my sunrise meditation in a quiet place in the university gardens, I *saw* and received the same current, quite unexpectedly, the same energy, the same feminine fluid coming from the sun, through its rays. It only lasted a few seconds, but what a surprise! I was far from thinking that such a thing was possible. What had happened had been tangible, and later on I came to believe that I had been given the opportunity to verify something the Master always said: love comes from on high and descends to the levels where we know it. It comes from the sun. The sun is its main distributor, and little by little it acquires lower vibrations to finally manifest itself on the etheric and then physical levels where we perceive it as attraction, including sexual attraction.

The beauty, the charm we see in a woman comes in fact from the sun. Love eventually condenses itself, benefiting this or that aspect of a woman, of a man. This was an incredible flash of insight, and I lived it in my cells. That experience, that gift, allowed me to carry on my quest about love, attempting to comprehend it in a different way than most of us do. Naturally, there were some downfalls, but one gets up again. Knowing that love can be experienced at yet unknown degrees is an incentive to move towards a light shining ahead.

I believe in an era to come, hopefully soon, in which all humanity will live in love, by way of love, a love so pure that it bestows upon life the fragrance of the Golden Age. This love is earned through experiences and sufferings, for temptations are indeed present, all kinds of temptations to fall back on the *conventional* understanding, whereas reality is so far above and beyond this. The Master used to say that the great Initiates no longer need to find love through a partner. They are able to feed night and day on the purest and most exquisite love in all of nature. They live constantly in love, which is a state of consciousness. It is not found outside of us, but within. Before attaining it, there are so many paths to travel, so much old baggage to leave by the wayside, and so many lifetimes necessary to attain it! But after all, the important thing is to know for sure where we want to go, so as not to indulge in so-called *normality*. Life is so infinite that we can only wish to discover and live ever more abundantly.

There have been times, of course, when waves of discouragement have overwhelmed me; times I have felt so worthless and small! Once, this lasted for several days, and it was one of the Master's books, *Freedom, the Spirit Triumphant,* that helped me enormously. It had just been released from the publishing house, Prosveta, and it helped me understand that, whatever the present situation we are facing, good or difficult, we have at our disposal all the tools necessary to create our future. The present is the fruit of the past, already crystallized, but with our mind sustained by our imagination, we can build our future. This is a fantastic key, holding out amazing hope for each of us! I held on tight to that idea and was able to overcome that difficult phase.

All the methods given by the Master (they are numerous, and every lecture contains many of them) are found in nature, which gave me a chance to better apprehend them and to foresee their possible use. Concrete images helped me a great deal to understand the mechanism of the universe, the laws and their operation, and to keep a link with what I already knew on the physical plane.

One of the joys I felt in joining this spiritual teaching was finding a resonance with what I felt when I was a child. When we are little, many of us think everything is alive. We speak to objects, flowers and animals, and we may even see little fairies at work or at play in nature. We sense many things without questioning them intellectually. Unfortunately, the adult world hurries to rid us of these predispositions, without knowing what lies behind them. Everything is actually alive; all of this is truly real.

A genuine spiritual teaching explains who the human being is, its true structure, its different bodies and souls (indeed, we have many souls!), and reveals methods to foster our most harmonious development in the different worlds in which we are immersed. It enables us, especially in these crucial times, to take part in the transformation of our beautiful planet and its inhabitants. Today's young people have many more possibilities and abilities than those of thirty years ago. Without guidance, models or criteria, they may feel lost in their search for themselves, not knowing who they are in a world that does not meet their aspirations. It would be wonderful if everyone became aware of the role he or she is meant to play in history's unfolding. The day we find our beacons, when light shines on our path, we will be able to dedicate our skills, our various gifts, to the service of this powerful wave of evolution that is carrying us all forward. We will then feel useful, participating in a grandiose work in which so many invisible beings are engaged, working for the Aquarian Age. This is a collective, fraternal work, ushering in a universal brotherhood in which we will no longer think solely of our own personal satisfaction (which is nothing more than mere illusion), but will be willing to serve a much vaster ideal.

Having had the good fortune, the privilege of knowing the Master in his physical incarnation, it fascinates me that a being with such knowledge, such wisdom and such power took on such a simple and humble appearance. He was always accessible, fraternal, manifesting an unconditional love and ever seeking to be useful to us. He advised us not to remain fixated on his physical presence, but showed us instead the sun as the model to follow. Master, my whole being says: "Thank you!"

Bertrand Lefèvre's biography:

As a teenager, I had a passion for the stars and built my own telescope. Then military service called me, after which I became a math/physics teacher in South America. From there, Canada had an appeal, and I spent one year in a research laboratory specializing in solar energy. Finally, I returned to France and settled in the sunny region of Provence. Having graduated from a renowned engineering institute, I have worked in an IT firm for 30 years.

CHAPTER 6

Interview with Carla Machado and Adolfo Leite

Can you describe one of your spiritual awakenings?

CARLA: My conscious awakening to the spiritual dimensions, my first mystical experience, happened when I was 21 years old, thanks to a book on Saint Francis of Assisi. I was by myself in my bedroom when I finished reading it and began singing a song with the words of his most well-known prayer. Suddenly a wonderful light filled the room. Thus began my interest in spiritual philosophy.

ADOLFO: A great Argentinean psychiatrist and psychotherapist friend of mine was the first person to convey to me an extraordinary and unified vision of the whole. I remember spending an entire day fasting without going hungry, nourished by a *different* kind of energy. A most vivid spiritual experience happened when I was 27 years old: my grandmother, who at the time was 89, had just suffered a stroke and was unconscious. I sat at her bedside about a yard away, with my palms facing towards her, fervently asking in the name of Jesus that she wake up. I distinctly sensed a strong current of energy flowing towards her through my hands. Two hours later, she recovered her senses and stayed an extra year and a half among us. I believe that I was instrumental in her full recovery, which had no after effects.

How did you discover the Teachings of Omraam Mikhaël Aïvanhov?

<u>CARLA</u>: The first time we heard of him was at a conference about prenatal life in Rio de Janeiro, in 2002. Being a mother and an astrologer, I immediately sensed the veracity of his tenets on the subject. During the following months, as I went on studying other aspects of his philosophy, I found more and more aspects that were of great interest to me, like the yoga of nutrition[33], the importance of each gesture, etc. Adolfo and I started adopting the Master's principles, and our lives became even more meaningful than it had been.

In the past, I had had some rather sad experiences while belonging to a spiritual movement, so I was cautious at first not to voice my interest in the Master's philosophy. But the depth and simplicity of what I found in his books caused my reluctance to gradually fade away.

<u>ADOLFO</u>: The first time we went to a center where people practice the teachings of the Master was in September 2008, for the Michaelmass celebration. We were in British Columbia, Canada, and after attending a prenatal psychology conference in Nelson, we drove in a hurry to that center nearby, so as to be on time for the fire ceremony. When we entered the property, a group of beautiful, galloping horses greeted us in the magic of dusk. The afternoon sky was welcoming the evening, and about 60 people were sitting around a pyramidal pile of wood ready to be lit. We sat down full of expectancy. The sister in charge lit the first branch, and soon the whole pile was on fire. Our three-year-old son commented that the fiery sparks were like stars in the sky. We

---

[33] Yoga of Nutrition, Izvor Collection # 204, Prosveta S.A. ISBN 978-85566-375-3

were contemplating the majestic flames when the brothers and sisters started singing the songs of the Brotherhood. "This must be Heaven!" I thought, deeply moved by this gathering of disciples, the gorgeous songs and the purity of their voices. An eagle circled above us and perched atop a pine tree nearby; I learned that it symbolized the Master's presence, pure and vigorous.

That evening, I realized that a society far less corrupted, simpler and fraternal is possible; I was witnessing a step in that direction. There were brothers and sisters from several countries; some had come from Bulgaria, others from the US, one was an expert in floral remedies from the Arctic regions, another a *dog whisperer* ... The serene and profound look in everyone's eyes spoke to me of eternity; the numinous quality in all of us was manifest. This experience was enchanting, especially in regard to the respect towards each other's inner time and dimensions! A seed, a living sample of what can come into being.

CARLA: The next day, we learned about the legend of Archangel Mikhael, how matter collaborates with spirit and how purity must be at the basis of everything we undertake, even at the basis of the sexual embrace. The Master's take on sexuality inspired many thoughts for me, and I was gifted with healing insights. I had already been in a spiritual retreat in India, and it was quite a different experience. As a whole, the people there are very religious, and in the ashram the energies are more oriented towards the guru. I did enjoy being in an ashram, especially taking part in the charitable activities for the poor, but at this Canadian center, the ambiance spoke of communion. I was thrilled to hear the voice of the Master for the first time. Once in a while, his throat would become scratchy, causing him to cough a little and drink some water; he explained that he was in fact transmuting negative energies coming from the audience ...

The generosity of this descended Master, who *shrunk* himself to inhabit a human body and bestowed on us such a grandiose Teaching, never ceases to amaze me! This fecund Teaching, exquisitely adapted to our level and our time in history ...

How did the Master's teachings impact your lives?

<u>CARLA</u>: The Master is for us like a safe haven, an oasis. His Teachings give a central axis to our daily lives, as their sound guiding parameters resonate with our core.

Every morning at home in São Paulo, we read out loud the Daily Meditation at breakfast. It *opens* our day with a spiritual balm, often bringing with it amazing synchronicities. Such soul proximity with the Master, his work and his disciples is sheer spiritual wealth for us.

One of the aspects of the Master's teachings that spoke to me the most is the importance of order. I had always had a taste for order, and the Master gave me one more reason to tidy up my bedroom before going to sleep: to welcome the visit of higher spiritual entities, their protection and their blessing.

<u>ADOLFO</u>: As a child, I was very fond of nature and animals, and I used to talk to God, imagining that I traveled to a land of utmost beauty and harmony, but with no human inhabitants. There, all the trees, flowers and plants were solely for the animals' sake. In his *Prayer for Harmony,* Master Omraam Mikhaël Aïvanhov instructs us to speak to the animals, telling them:

> When God first created the world, you lived in peace and harmony with man; we owe you some help because it is by our fault that you became cruel and have to survive under such difficult conditions. I send you light to help you advance rapidly on the path of evolution. [34]

[34] *A New Earth, Methods, exercises, formulas and prayers.* Complete Works, vol. 13, Prosveta S.A., p. 230. ISBN978-2-85566-622-8

Such words are music to my soul. I have now peopled this paradisiacal land of mine; the Master's lectures and his disciples certainly helped me understand how possible it is for us humans to become a civilization that strives for kinship with all life, where harmony and interspecies communication is the norm.

CARLA: We became vegetarian, and the Master's teachings brought us more joy, more consciousness at meal times. His *hrani yoga,*[35] or yoga of nutrition, enhanced our family's relationship with life by gifting us with the awareness of what happens to our food before it reaches our plate. Eating with thankfulness for the humans and the forces of nature which foster the growth of delicious fruits and vegetables certainly enhances the quality of digestion and our friendship with planet earth. It became more and more important for us to know the provenance of our food, and we joined a local CSA (Community Supported Agriculture), part of a worldwide movement that honors the farmer and his work, while respecting the soil and seeds and their unfathomable wisdom.

When our daughter was 16, she handwrote about ten pages from some of the Master's books—translating into Portuguese bits of paragraphs from the French, Spanish or English—in order to comfort and bring courage to a friend of hers who was feeling depressed.

Nowadays, Adolfo and I hold a meeting once a week in São Paulo at our home with a group of friends who wish to study the Teaching. These are informal gatherings: we read from a book of the Master and then comment on the joys and challenges we encounter as we strive to apply his wisdom in our daily lives. Several of the participants come from an anthroposophical background, and they delight in the joy and clarity of the Master's style.

---

[35] *Hrani yoga, The alchemical and magical meaning of nutrition*, Complete Works, Prosveta S.A., Vol. 16. ISBN978-2-85566-958-8

<u>ADOLFO</u>: The Paneurythmy was a great discovery for me, like a marvelous vision of angels dancing. It is a dance to share with the whole world! So, every Saturday morning, we join a group of Master Peter Deunov's disciples and dance it with them.

We traveled a few years ago to the south of France and spent a few days at the Bonfin. It wasn't during a congress, so the place was quite empty, but the brothers and sisters who live there all year long welcomed us with much warmth. A delicate and surreal fragrance of roses greeted us just outside the Master's chalet.

<u>CARLA</u>: We went up the hill to the *Rocher*, just outside the Bonfin, and I was suddenly transported to a time when hundreds of people were meditating there! Their backs were straight and attentive. At the very front I could see the Master, and in the horizon the first rays of the sun were spreading their radiant light. This vision was, and still is, a blessed confirmation of my path.

<u>ADOLFO</u>: I somehow knew that we are of a divine nature, and I had always considered water as a sacred entity embodying life and purity, beckoning us to enter deeper levels of reality. The Master confirmed this intuitive knowledge of mine and helped me to further decipher the divine within us, the exquisite intelligence of each and every cell in our body. The grand but subtle holographic tapestry he wove into his Teachings comes together with a force of transformation and beckons us to explore and discover the ways of Cosmic Intelligence.

<u>CARLA</u>: I became very involved with the Master's teachings about the power of a pregnant woman's inner life[36]. It moved me immensely, and years later, when I was invited to create an ANEP (National Association for Prenatal Education) in Brazil, I asked

---

[36] *Hope for the World: Spiritual Galvanoplasty*, Izvor Collection, #214, Prosveta S.A. ISBN 978-1-895978-14-8

the Master inwardly one night before falling asleep whether to accept the invitation or not. That same night I dreamt of him. In the dream, my husband and I were in our bedroom, and the Master kept looking into our eyes with serenity, but intently. Needless to say, I readily accepted the post, already sensing how important and all-encompassing this endeavor would become for me, of course, but also for my friends and family. It has been a joy to head the ANEP Brazil during these last six years and to contribute to a local, nationwide and worldwide dissemination of its mighty principles for more fraternal societies around the globe.

ADOLFO: The Master stressed how children learn by imitation and reminded parents to be worthy of their children's imitation. The path of conscious parenting kindled my interest in Waldorf pedagogy, in which the teacher must know his or her own inner child in order to stay away from projections and their pitiful ravages. Rudolf Steiner explained in his very first conference to teachers in 1919 that true teachers don't teach alone: they are conduits for the spiritual world through which special entities come and teach. To teach is to nurture the blossoming of what each student came to do on earth, by helping to develop his or her most luminous skills. Nevertheless, classrooms often end up feeling more like a jail than a place where one's consciousness gains a solid understanding of the values pertaining to the subject being taught. No wonder Master Omraam revealed that the highest, most sacred profession is that of the teacher!

CARLA: Since childhood, I had felt a strong attraction towards the sun, but was brought up to enjoy sleeping until late. The Master's *Solar Religion*[37] changed that: I am today a morning person, loving dawn, sensing the life and force in the very first rays of the sun. When I read about it, it had the ring of truth, sounded good and brought me great joy. The whole world needs

---

[37] *A Solar Civilization*, Izvor Collection #201, Prosveta S.A. ISBN 978-85566-373-9

to know about this! I loved learning, for instance, that we radiate thoughts which reach other minds and then come back to us one day, the same way the sun radiates its rays and eventually gets them back.

During my second pregnancy, I went to the sun in my meditations; that prodigious star was for me a primary source of inspiration. And my son was born blond, in spite of the fact that my husband and I—as well as our respective families— have very dark hair! At the age of three he would tell me while stroking his hair, "Mom, my hair shines like rays of sunshine ... "

Carla Machado's and Adolfo Leite's biography:

- ❖ *Carla Machado left the corporate world following the birth of her first child, having worked for 12 years as a system analyst at IBM. She chose to dedicate more time to motherhood and to the arrival of new humans on the planet. Today she is the President of ANEP Brazil (National Association for Prenatal Education) and OMAEP's vice- president (World Organization of the Associations for Prenatal Education). She is a psychotherapist, an astrologer and a facilitator of experiential and philosophical workshops for groups.*
- ❖ *For the last 25 years, Adolfo Leite has been working at IBM, mostly in the Human Resources department. He is a father, an acupuncturist, and is trained in Waldorf pedagogy.*

CHAPTER 7

Laura's journey

With Master Omraam Mikhaël Aïvanhov, I learned that the universe is both intelligent and intelligible. He introduced me to the field of consciousness, a realm in which authenticity reigns and where imagination and intuition are our guides. My feelings towards him are those of infinite gratitude.

During a summer vacation, while visiting my parents in Algiers where they were assigned as Brazilian diplomats, a Peruvian shaman and diplomat gave me two brochures by Omraam. I was 22 years old. I didn't even know I had a soul, and my spiritual nature was certainly starving.

One of the brochures was entitled *Le Sacrifice*. Its style was direct, its content exceptionally insightful, and I was pleased to encounter a philosophy, a wisdom crafted for all—not just for the intellectually primed. How could this author grab my interest, line after line, exploring such a daunting realm? How did he manage to make the subject of sacrifice an enticing invitation to perfect myself? He rocked my boat, and I wanted more.

The second brochure was about the sun. In it Omraam explained how each of its first rays is like wagons filled with goods for the new day, and that it is up to us to receive these blessed victuals. The sunrise? A daily event within everyone's reach is a magical cauldron of golden riches? I had to smile, as this surely couldn't be possible ... yet my whole being was already trusting Omraam's vision.

Twenty days after receiving these brochures, I sensed that my being on earth was about to acquire a whole new dimension. It was September 1976, and at the time only thirteen books had been published. I read them all, thirsty for their nurturing explanations, fascinated by Omraam's ability to impart profound concepts with such clarity, and perplexed at the fact that I hadn't encountered anything like this before.

Angels and archangels, reincarnation, entities of the four elements, the powers of thought, the solar plexus, the spiritual forces inherent in lovemaking, how to relate to food, the inhabitants of our inner world, and many other themes—all new to me—began to permeate my mind, composing a fascinating holographic tapestry. It all seemed worth applying and living for: here finally was a road map for my existence. It was up to me to study its geography, climb its mountains, navigate its waters, walk its forests and prairies, explore its caves ... Life made so much sense, and I was filled with joy!

At the end of the second volume, I read two chapters in which Omraam addressed the power of a pregnant mother's imagination and asked the reader to spread the news to expectant mothers near and far. Quite a counterculture request at a time when mainstream science was marred with genetic determinism, but I committed to do just that: to tell every pregnant woman I would meet about the enormous and lasting impact she has over her child's development.

Came Christmas day, I met the Master in Sèvres, a suburb of Paris. He gave an enthralling talk on Egyptian initiation, and after lunch, while we were in meditation, we heard a superb recording of Beethoven's Missa Solemnis. All of this was a first for me, a magnificent first! His presence was vast, his words edifying and inspiring, his smile welcoming. In college I had studied experimental psychology. With him I was learning spiritual psychology: how to invite the sublime into my daily life.

In the evening, I went to see my parents who were spending some days in Paris. Over dinner I told them about the Master, expressed my joy at studying his Teachings, and showed them one of his books. Red flags went up in their minds. They had never expected my life to take a spiritual turn and feared losing me to a sect. I saw sadness in their eyes. Nothing I could say seemed to soothe their concern. Their only hope was that I would soon come to my senses and go back to relying solely on the powers of the intellect to guide my life. For them, as for many of their social status, spirituality was at most a *side dish*, a symbolic way to pay tribute to the unfathomable. Esotericism was out of the question. I met the philosophical divergences with my parents in a tranquil manner, saddened to be worrying them, but resolute in my intention to welcome spirituality into my life. Peacefully facing their disapproval triggered valuable resources in me; I acquired more resilience and began to be less of a *pleaser*, which to this day helps me in many instances of rejection by the *status quo*.

Since 1938, Omraam had been stressing how civilizations thrive or plummet according to the quality of their pregnant mothers' imagination. I felt ready for a lifetime *backstage*, whispering to pregnant women how nature had entrusted them with the means and responsibility to educate their 'prenates' for a fulfilling adulthood. As I then saw it in 1976, a whole century would probably go by before scientists would begin to consider a pregnant mother's power and discover how much her inner life influences the configuration of her baby's neural pathways. I was ninety years wrong. In the 1980s, psychologists began pondering ideas related to the early constructs of the human mind, and prenatal psychology was born.[38] In the 1990s, biochemistry and cell biology took a transformative leap, landing the wonders of prenatal life in the scientific arena: *center stage!*

---

[38] APPPAH Association for Prenatal & Perinatal Psychology and Health www.birthpsychology.com

On a joyous morning, just after sunrise meditation on the *Rocher*[39] at the Bonfin, I was introduced to a brother from the United States. We became friends on the spot and in the years following saw each other several times at the Bonfin. We then had a fortuitous encounter in Los Angeles and were married several months later. Getting acquainted with the path of consciousness as a couple was a fascinating undertaking. Now there were two of us striving to apply the Master's teachings and manifest in our day-to-day lives what we understood about the soulful privilege of being on earth. We shared the same enthusiasm for Omraam's powerful insights into conscious conception and conscious pregnancy, so when I became pregnant we felt truly blessed. I remembered Omraam explaining that good nutrition is paramount for a pregnant mother, that without it, the baby's brain doesn't fully develop, and her offspring will have a faulty *instrument* for this incarnation. Also, how she lives, the way she feels about herself, about others and about the universe all contribute indelibly to the formation of her baby.[40] Indeed, her enthusiasm and her joy as well as her anguish and sorrows constantly *feed* the development of the baby's every organ and system.

Throughout millennia, esoteric traditions have taught that the womb is our first and most important school, where we receive a thorough education about how to live and grow according to our mother's *lessons*. Omraam had often described to us an extraordinary vision in which governments would assign important resources to the creation of gorgeous parks where pregnant mothers could spend their pregnancy in health, joy, beauty and harmony. Thus, all over the world people would begin to change from the inside out. He estimated that as a result, within 50 years prisons and psychiatric hospitals would

---

[39] The Rocher is the rock of prayer where brothers and sisters gather for the sunrise.

[40] *Education begins before Birth* and *Hope for the World, Spiritual Galvanoplasty*, Prosveta S.A Izvor Collection #203 and #214.

begin to close their doors. I cherish this vision; its genius never ceases to impress me. He knew of the blissful synergy among pregnant bellies, how the forces of health prefer to work in a harmonious ambiance, and how a brand new physical body is much better formed when the pregnant mother feels hopeful, serene and inspired.

When I was pregnant, I had it all: I traveled, sang, meditated at sunrise, read fabulous books, ate well and felt inspired. But in spite of such privileges, I yearned for one of these parks of beauty, for the joy of togetherness with many other pregnant mothers, for singing, swimming, painting, reading, writing, taking walks, embroidering, stargazing with them ... and although my pregnancy was wonderful, I understood even more profoundly the value of these seminal parks. Science now understands that the psychological and biological *moods* in which we are formed in the womb remain stored in our subliminal memory, forever echoing in us. Indeed, our prenatal neurophysiological development becomes a lasting reference for the way we experience life. So when Omraam associates evils like pollution, corruption, drug addiction, depression and social injustice to inadequate formation in the womb, he conveys great news: transform once and for all the physical and psychological environment in which women live their pregnancies, and they will begin to birth more robust, resilient, creative and fraternal human beings. Three generations later, he said, creatures of *gold*—incorruptible—will people our nations, with women and men able to put an end to the many ills that compromise our kinship with all life.

Most of our leaders throughout history have tended to choose war over brotherhood, injustice over social inclusion, rivalry over collaboration, cruelty over empathy, depletion over sustainability. And a look throughout history at how so many ruling families were founded, how pregnant women were considered, how their children were breastfed—often by wet-nurses—sheds a galaxy of light on why so many of these leaders grew up to be self-centered and insecure. In order to feel powerful, they had to demean, conquer, control and betray; their self-esteem was low, their brain circuitry incomplete—poor in mirror neurons and serotonin receptors. Omraam made it very clear in countless lectures that as long as life in the womb is not optimized for each and every one of us, even the most brilliant socio-economic reforms will end up sabotaged by anguish, envy, fear, pessimism, mistrust, self-aggrandizement, cruelty ... Humanity's only hope is to foster the well-being of our pregnant women.

Moreover, according to this great spiritual Master, we are each pregnant with our tomorrow's self, physically and psychologically. Yes, even for those of us who are not expecting a baby, our inner environment is central to our wellbeing. Our hopes, joys, discernment and altruism—or lack thereof—endlessly orchestrate our neurophysiology. Our thoughts, feelings and actions are continuously translated into our blood biochemistry, conveying their very nature to our trillions of cells. How we live, what we read, the ideas we value and our moods contribute to the nature of our future self. What a program, what a prodigious responsibility! Omraam offers a great tip for our future health: the quality of our gestures—graceful or clumsy, mindful or impatient, conscious or on automatic pilot—models how our cells will treat each other.

For 50 years, Omraam spoke about universal spiritual principles and laws. His lectures offer a myriad of exercises to choose from, according to our affinities and capabilities. What captivates me, for instance, are his revelations about the four elements—earth, water, air and fire—and their correspondences with our actions, emotions, thoughts and spiritual life. The possibility of communing with their wisdom had never crossed my mind! To perceive these building blocks of our world as representatives of mighty spiritual entities, to know we can converse with them and be helped by them, changed and enriched me.

For Omraam, inner sovereignty is a constant quest. Inner challenges and tests became my travelling companions on the path of consciousness. Back in the autumn of 1976, I purposely began to see things as if for the very first time. Trees, skies, flowers, food ... all of these became invitations to marvel and revere. I wanted to learn everything from scratch, even how to eat. Chewing on a delicious apple while breathing deeply, welcoming it within me, grateful for its savor, curious about its experience, aware that its tree knows much more than I do, inviting it to share its understanding of the universe with my cells ... this yoga of nutrition, which Omraam named *Hrani yoga*, radically transformed my way of eating.

And there were songs: choral singing is another gift the Master brought us. Songs in Bulgarian, composed by his spiritual Master Peter Deunov, enchant my life to this day. I found out that my voice is *alto*, and I was assigned rehearsals with the alto group.

These were the beginnings of great friendships, and still today, the joy of sharing a spiritual path with like-minded students of the sublime enhances my every day with meaningful exchanges. My burgeoning understanding of esotericism allows me to work side by side with audacious weavers of a better world.

The danger? To revert to automatic pilot, to take life's beauty, generosity and intelligence for granted, as something commonplace.

One of my greatest thrills was discovering that throughout the ages a perennial philosophy had always been accessible to all those who wanted to study the essence of life, the purpose of being here on earth. To know that a person like me can travel from British Columbia to southern Chile and back via South Africa, France, Italy and the UK meeting all sorts of students of this universal spiritual philosophy is exhilarating! In my travels I meet new friends, and Omraam's philosophy enables me to celebrate the beauty of many lives. The gift of friendship comes with his Teaching, not only friendship with specific human beings, but also with trees, stars, flowers, mountains and animals, friendship with ideas and with the entities of other realms ...

I have also experienced how consciousness eases the challenges of parenting, even rendering them enjoyable. Regarding a child's upbringing, Omraam reminded his students of sound principles. For instance, children learn by example, and *who-we-are* is what actually counts for them, a beckoning invitation to perfect ourselves, to master our inner lives. As for my parents, well, they recovered: some twenty years later they came to terms with having a daughter who had chosen to study spirituality. What I most admire in them is that they always welcomed me, even when they downright disagreed with my choices.

Almost forty years after having met him, I am still in awe of Omraam's wisdom, generosity and enthusiasm. A fabulous Ambassador from Heaven, he tirelessly unveiled the workings of Cosmic Intelligence. For him, the famous Old Testament phrase *grow and multiply* is in fact an invitation to further elaborate creation with life. I have been privileged to witness his ardent dedication to humanity's spiritual enfolding. It is humbling to write about him, and I cannot do him justice.

Year after year, his wisdom is increasingly more accessible, now available in many languages and many forms—books, videos, CDs, the Internet, etc.—to all seekers.

As I write these lines, countless associations champion the cause of women in labor and their basic needs. Breastfeeding is better understood than ever before, and an increasing number of parents are awakening to the joys of closely accompanying the first years of their children's lives and nurturing their spiritual nature. Although the number of proponents of prenatal life is steadily growing, parks dedicated to beauty and harmony for pregnant mothers have yet to be devised. I wonder which nation will be the first to understand the relevance of investing in their well-being. Perhaps art will galvanize the will of nations and their governments. Perhaps a great novel, a play, an epic motion picture about the powerful influences of prenatal life will inspire large audiences worldwide, will touch the hearts of many and launch the construction of centers for pregnant mothers everywhere on earth.

Meanwhile, schools and universities should include in their curricula this critical understanding of how our life in the womb shapes who we become, and how this *cellular education* that precedes our arrival on earth is essential to how we behave throughout our adult years. I lecture on these themes at the University of Concepción, Chile, and at a University in Perugia, Italy. Similar programs also exist online from Greece and the United States. For now, however, this precious body of knowledge is available to the very few, leaving the vast majority to consider pregnancy merely as a preparation for motherhood, instead of a most vital period of education.

I invite you to spread the news about the extraordinary power of a woman when she is carrying a baby—a future citizen of our planet—in her womb.

Laura Uplinger's biography:

Laura is a proponent and educator in the field of conscious conception and prenatal and perinatal parenting. Fluent in four languages, she bridges several cultures, traveling between Europe and the Americas as a featured speaker for parents, high school and college students, birth professionals and psychotherapists.

- International Foundation Omraam Villa de Vico Onlus: www.fondazioneomraam.org/UK/index.html
- Journey with Omraam: http://with-omraam.com/

ADDENDUM BY LAURA UPLINGER

As an example of my contribution to Omraam's plan, here is *Childbirth in 4012*, a text I wrote in October, 2012, for the Mid-Pacific Conference on Birth and Primal Health Research in Honolulu. It was the title that Dr. Michel Odent, its organizer, had assigned to the closing roundtable.

Childbirth in 4012

The times we enjoy today in 4012 were only a utopian vision in previous civilizations. For millennia, love had been diseased— both love of self as well as love for others. That essential kernel of self-esteem had never been collectively addressed and nurtured; it had never truly blossomed in any nation. Yes, throughout the ages there had been individuals whose hearts and minds had flourished without ever betraying life, who were prone to kinship with all. But they were not many.

Prisons were full. Abuse, betrayal, greed, war, crime and indifference were common plagues among governing elites. Always a foul thirst to diminish and control others in order to feel better.

However, towards the end of the 20th century and into the first decades of the 21st, diverse branches of science shed galaxies of light on the genesis of a wholly healthy human being, confirming what many sacred wisdom traditions had taught since the dawn of time.

The intricate physiological orchestration of our development in the womb was finally understood, appreciated and respected! Babies were given better and better conditions in which to grow and develop robust and resilient organs—especially the brain—thanks to an optimal biochemistry and the nutrients flowing in their mother's blood.

In schools and universities, students of all ages learned about nature's plan for a fulfilling primal period. All over the world, governments began waking up to the simple yet grand reality that every pregnant woman needs above all to eat well, to feel joy and to be inspired by beauty.

For the first time in over 12,000 years, societies began dedicating important financial and cultural resources to the well-being of pregnant women, in order to protect this decisive stage of parenting. For the first time in all those millennia, the powers that be got it: mothers birth civilizations.

The 21st century saw the inception of the centers we enjoy today in cities, suburbs, and remote villages: gathering places built in gorgeous parks where expectant mothers walk in nature, sing together, rest, weave, paint, read, dance, swim, enjoying an exquisite and joyful synergy among the wee inhabitants of their pregnant bellies.

As humanity learned how receptive we are to the inner world of our parents, that the integrity of our adult body and its trillions of cells begins in the loving nature of their sexual embrace, unplanned pregnancies became increasingly rare. Even the months leading up to conception began to be consciously lived.

Oh, and I have to tell you about birth! The ignorance that had marred most birth practices slowly receded and died. The unbridled use of technological intervention—finally recognized as counterproductive at best and abusive at worst—peaked in the early 21st century. Once and for all, "experts" left laboring mothers undisturbed, trusting their bodies' wisdom. Quiet and privacy were embraced as the primary facilitators of easy childbirth.

The decade of the 2050s marked a turning point when the first generation of the wellborn attained maturity. They grew up to be teachers, artists, merchants and policy makers of a different breed. Their presence on earth instilled more creativity, empathy, flexibility, social intelligence and resilience into the marrow of the human family.

They began to have their own children, and the benefits of investing in primal health were revealed to be exponential improvements across generations. People lived longer and enjoyed greater well-being. Breastfeeding became an uncontested and universal practice as wet nurses and formula faded into oblivion. Prisons, psychiatric hospitals and NICUs (neonatal intensive care units) began closing their doors. Artificial borders between nations were declared obsolete.

Well, this is how we reached the Golden Age our ancestors so deeply longed for and worked so tirelessly to realize.

POSTFACE

Although Hubert Mansion is not a member of the Aquarian Team, he is a valued friend who wrote a text perfectly suited for our book, and we are happy to share with you here.

THE WORLD NEEDS HAPPY PEOPLE

It happened some twenty years ago …

A friend had slipped into my coat pocket a little book, which I barely glanced at and subsequently forgot about. Not long after that, my life changed drastically, with unexpected difficulties sweeping away in a gust of wind everything that only the day before had seemed stable and deeply rooted.

That day I found myself in a park, attempting to take stock of the storm I was passing through.

It was early April and still cold. Plunging my hand in my pocket, I felt this little volume and took it out. Its title read *The Powers of Thought* by Omraam Mikhaël Aïvanhov, a name completely unfamiliar to me. Continuing to walk in the park amidst a scattering of pigeons, I imagined I would probably find in it those ready-made 'spiritual' phrases I had read a thousand times: 'tomorrow is a new day', 'meet life with a smile', 'open your heart to joy', 'rediscover your inner child', all illustrated with pink and blue drawings perfectly designed to further depress me. So I randomly opened the book, ready to toss it into the first available trash can at the slightest hint of sentimentality.

The first paragraph stunned me, and I almost fell to the frozen ground with astonishment.

Not only did I discover in these pages a kind of confirmation of something that, deep within me, I already knew, but both the abstract and concrete dimension of the Teaching before my eyes enabled me to put into action immediately the lines I had just read. In only a few seconds, my view of the world changed, not completely, of course; perhaps it moved only a fraction of an inch from its former perspective. But the move was permanent and enough to create a complete revolution against my mental inertia and became one of the greatest blessings of my life.

Thinking back on it, I can still feel the sensations I experienced at the time. I see myself working that cold night on my thinking, changing its orientation, inwardly resetting my sails, trying out all the methods proposed. I who had read all the philosophers, the thinkers, the ancients and the moderns, who had spent thousands of hours seeking answers in complicated reports, found myself in the face of a disarming, even disturbing simplicity. And I remember saying to myself: why wasn't I taught this in school? I only had the answer fifteen years later ...

When we buy a cabinet at Ikea, it comes with planks and directions. But no one tells us what to do if we aren't handy, if we lose a screw, if we begin to get irritated, if someone comments on our incredible ineptitude and we feel like throwing the whole project out the window ... since one of the roles of matter, according to Omraam Mikhaël Aïvanhov, is to resist spirit (which it certainly does in my case). We are given the instructions, but there is no instructor.

The teaching of Omraam Mikhaël Aïvanhov is, on the contrary, that of an instructor. Having consecrated his entire life to 'elevating' himself, to transforming himself, then to guiding thousands of people on this path, he knows all the tools, because he has used them. "Spirituality, he said, is knowing how to make use of every kind of work to elevate oneself, to harmonize oneself, to link oneself with Heaven." This includes everything: respiration, thought, nutrition, sexuality, gardening, language, exercise, chemistry, music, economy, actions, beauty and ugliness, good and evil, poverty and wealth, politics, motherhood, pedagogy ... What use in fact is spirituality if it amounts only to an ideal? We all know what we should be. We need no one to indicate our destination, because we can envision it, as individuals and as a society.

But how are we to arrive there, how are we to attain this goal? And what are we to do right now, in the next moment? This is the great question—the question of the twenty-first century—which, in its collective consciousness no longer ponders, the legitimacy of war, of slavery, of violence as it did one hundred years ago. If we continue daily to denounce the atrocities in the world, we must not conclude that in effect they are growing, but rather that practices that appeared admissible in other times appear scandalous today.

The question is not what to do, but how to do it.

Among the great spiritual Teachings, that of Omraam Mikhaël Aïvanhov is distinguished by the extraordinary quantity of practical and concrete methods proposed for attaining the goal we know of. In fact there are so many of these methods in the thousands of lectures given, that he himself asked that we not use all of them, but choose those which suit us.

I have used a great number of them. For example, when I am feeling sad, I light the lights within me: I imagine my body full of paper lanterns and I light them one by one, transforming myself into a Christmas tree at night. Almost immediately this changes my inner state. I have recharged myself by touching trees; I have used words that possess great power; I have tried fasting; I have learned to master my gaze, my gestures. In order to feel happier, I have exploited the resources of my imagination, my thought, my gestures, and this has completely transformed my existence. I am far from being a frontrunner, but I have traveled a long distance.

One must not work to make the world happy, but to become happy oneself. To do so is a necessity, an absolute duty. The power to change the world belongs only to those who have changed themselves, because they have overcome their individual human inertia, which is the cause of so much suffering. It is no longer time to create happiness for others in spite of themselves, but to create happiness for oneself in spite of the world, and in doing so to transform the world.

The world today needs happy people!

Hubert Mansion's biography:

Born in Belgium of musician parents, he came to Quebec in the year 2000. A former lawyer specialized in entertainment law with an international clientele, administrator of the world heritage of Maurice Maeterlinck (Nobel Prize in Literature, Belgium), author of numerous works, founder of the University in Nature, he is also a well-known international speaker.

ACKNOWLEDGEMENTS

The Aquarian Team would like to give thanks with all their heart to those who have contributed to the editing and final reading of our second book: Laura, Shannon and Penny. All authors, editors and reviewers have donated their valuable time and skills. Moreover, the authors have agreed to donate all profits from the book sales to charitable organizations.

Invitation:

We invite you to visit our website for updates and news about the team: www.TheAquarianTeam.com, and to like our Facebook page: The Aquarian Team.

You may also request to be added to the subscribers list for our inspiring, free monthly e-newsletter at: newsletter@ theaquarianteam.com

References:

Books and DVDs: www.Prosveta.com (with references in many languages)

Universal White Brotherhood:
http://www.fbu.org/site_anglais/general_english/name.htm

Lectures of Omraam Mikhaël Aïvanhov on YouTube: www.youtube.com/watch?v=BxCy2GjZKxw

Information and worldwide study sessions on the life and Teaching of Omraam Mikhaël Aïvanhov: www.with-omraam.com

ABOUT THE AUTHORS

The journeys composing this book is the fruit of a team effort: eight authors and three proofreaders/editors who worked together to make it ripe. The authors have opened their heart and their life to share with you the journey of their soul. Along their path they discovered the teachings of Omraam Mikhaël Aïvanhov which contributed immensely to their growth and blossoming. They hope that your heart will be touched and your soul inspired by their stories.

Claude Brun, Sally Huss, Mark Walker, Bertrand Lefèvre, Carla Machado, Adolfo Leite, Laura Uplinger and Carmen Froment as the coordinator and copyright holder of the book.

Printed in the United States
By Bookmasters